GIFT

AND

GRIT

How Heroic Virtue Can Change
Your Life and Relationships

ANDREW *and*
SARAH SWAFFORD

ASCENSION

West Chester, Pennsylvania

Ascension
PO Box 1990
West Chester, PA 19380
1-800-376-0520
ascensionpress.com

Cover design: Faceout Studio

Printed in the United States of America
23 24 25 26 27 5 4 3 2 1

ISBN 978-1-954881-91-4 (paperback)
ISBN 978-1-954881-93-8 (e-book)

We dedicate this book with love and affection
to our Florence students, our *Środowisko*.

With fondness, we also remember all those with whom we have been
able to share the life and teachings of St. John Paul II and all those who
have shared his life and teachings with us—we are forever grateful.

CONTENTS

PART V: LIVING GIFT AND GRIT IN RELATIONSHIP WITH GOD

PART I
WHY WE WROTE
THIS BOOK

INTRODUCTION

We have been walking with college students and young adults for over fifteen years, and we absolutely love it! *Sarah:* When I wrote my book *Emotional Virtue: A Guide to Drama-Free Relationships*, it was truly the fruit of my time as a residence hall director at Benedictine College. Living in the dorm gave me and my husband (whom I affectionately call "Swaff") an extraordinary, up close view into students' lives. We would listen and ask questions and try to process all that these men and women were telling us—and then we would take our faith, formation, and compassion for their plight and try to help in any way we could. As much as I would love to go to coffee with every student at Benedictine (and with young people all over the country), *Emotional Virtue* was a way of sharing the advice that we kept giving over and over again, especially with those we might never be able to chat with face-to-face around our kitchen island.

Our three years in the dorm just happened to be the same years that social media came on the scene, along with the newfound popularity of smartphone texting and FaceTime. It is hard for most of us to even remember a time when these things did not exist. But we remember vividly trying to help our students sort through these new forms of communication—especially when it came to navigating the dating scene and the inevitable "gray areas" of "Oh, we're just talking, texting, hanging out." We saw firsthand how these new forms of social media led to a dramatic increase in confusion, uncertainty, and insecurity surrounding dating relationships.

Social media has changed a lot since then, and it continues to evolve. One of the gifts of teaching at Benedictine and living across the street from more than two thousand college students is that we meet new young men and women every year. While the students change as they face new challenges dealing with new forms of social media, underneath it all, their struggles are still very much the same.

They are the fundamental human struggles we all face. Over the years, we often hear things like:

I feel isolated, but I don't want to be alone.

I put on a brave face, but inside I am sad and insecure; I have fears that I can't even articulate.

I don't have good friends, and I don't know how to make good friends.

I'm tired and exhausted by the demands of life.

I feel disappointed, and bitterness seems to be creeping in.

I am scared to fail, and it is humiliating to admit my weaknesses—to anybody.

I want to learn how to really talk to people, but it can be difficult to communicate in person.

I don't have direction in my life. I feel aimless, confused, and anxious.

Sometimes I feel worthless, and I don't believe I'll ever be "enough."

I want to make an impact on the world, but I don't know where to start.

This list could go on and on. In a world of perfectionism, competition, and status seeking (in real life as well as on a screen), it is almost impossible not to be affected by what can feel like an all-out assault on who we are and our sense of self-worth. It is so easy to fall prey to self-doubt, especially when we succumb to the "comparison game," a sure thief of our peace and joy.

In our quiet moments, sometimes we face the deep questions of life, which can be haunting and overwhelming, questions such as:

Who am I?

What am I living for?

Who am I living for?

Why do I do what I do?

Why don't I do what I want or need to do?

What gives my life meaning?

Is it worth the fight?

Am I worth the fight?

Who do I want to be? Who am I called to be?

What holds me back from the person I want to be?

It can all feel so heavy. But it is worth reflecting deeply on these questions, even if we might want to push them away and ignore them.

Life is a journey, and *we are becoming a certain kind of person along the way.* All the little decisions we make every day—all the countless thoughts that run through our minds—slowly form us into who we are. These patterns and habits (whether we realize it or not) eventually become our most honest answers to the big questions of life—of who we truly are and where we are going.

We saw this up close when we were asked by Benedictine to teach a semester abroad at its campus in Florence, Italy. We packed up our four children at the time and traveled with forty-eight Benedictine students to Europe for a three-month adventure. While we have always enjoyed spending time with our students, living in such close quarters with them was truly unique—sharing meals (and lots of gelato!), going on long train rides, and residing in the same villa.

Since we were removed from the typical pressures of daily life, we were really able to share our lives with them—and they shared their hearts with us. We were able to walk with them in a very special way. *Sarah:* I remember looking at Swaff, saying, "What they are carrying is heavy. And it looks different from what we dealt with in college, and even different from what the students dealt with when we were back in the dorms." Over the next three months, we walked with them and listened to their stories and their questions; we listened as they opened up about their wounds, their fears, their hopes, their shame, and their deep desire for wholeness and happiness. Through this, we all became very close. It was truly life changing in so many ways.

This book is an attempt to share with others what made that semester so special. In some ways, it captures the unique connection that emerged between the extraordinary openness of our students and the formation we were offering them as we tried to support them in whatever way we could.

Our students walked away from that trip changed; and so did we.

New friendships formed (with some even turning into marriages!), and a great many encountered Jesus Christ in a way that altered the course of their lives forever.

Sometimes a teacher or youth minister or priest is blessed to touch people's lives in profound ways, sometimes even making a deep and life-changing impact. This is what happened to us when we were in college, and it is the reason why we seek to give back in the same way that people gave so generously to us.

But that semester, *our students also formed us.*

As our trip was coming to an end, some of our students asked if we would meet to recap the semester and answer questions. They especially wanted to know: "How do we take this home? How do we live out our faith—and continue in these profound friendships—in the freedom and joy we have found here?"

This was a good question. These students would soon return to friends and even family who had not experienced these life-changing months abroad. How would they explain what happened? Would they be supported? Or would they meet resistance? If so, how should they handle it?

So, the night before we left Florence, we planned a get-together to take questions and discuss their concerns. Initially, we expected only a handful of students to come.

What happened next truly astounded us.

Every student showed up. We spent several hours with them—sharing stories, laughing, crying, and talking about how to bring what happened in Florence back home with us. Everyone in that room had a firm resolve not to let what happened abroad die there. And this resolve has only continued, as these friendships (both among the students and between our family and the students) have flourished ever since.

This book, though, is not really about Florence. The things we were sharing, teaching, and passing on as we lived with these young people for those three months were the same things we have been sharing for more than a decade—everything just happened faster in Florence, as we got to know those students so well and so quickly. We were able to see firsthand the explosive connection between *where our students were at* and *the way of life we were sharing with them*. While there was something unrepeatable about that semester, this book is an effort to share this experience with others. And since the struggles of our students are ultimately no different from those of anybody else (at any age or stage in life), what happened in Florence will find deep resonance and relevance for many others.

The energy of that semester in Florence revealed something special—it uniquely illumined the human condition as manifest in our time; and it showcased the transformative power of the Gospel to reach people precisely where they are.

Whether it is the students who were with us in Florence or those we have been walking with for more than a decade, they often tell us things like:

"I needed someone to give it to me straight. I needed someone to love me enough to challenge me, and to still love me when I fail."

"I needed someone to answer my questions and not sugarcoat it. I needed someone to show me how to be friends with the opposite sex."

"I needed someone to speak into my brokenness and tell me that I am not alone. I needed someone to help me hope in love again."

"I needed someone to show me why faith is important and how to build my life around it. I needed someone to walk with me. I needed to know that someone cared."

We tried to do this for our students—and, through this book, we hope to do the same for you. We wrote this book because we care. We care about you, and we are deeply passionate (and sympathetic) about the tremendous battles you face and all that you are up against—which seems only to get more difficult with each passing year.

Think of us as an older brother and sister who will be honest with you and want to go to battle with you and for you in this game of life. You are loved and worth fighting for; our desire is for you to be whole, happy, free, and at peace. When we walk with people, we often say, "This won't always be easy, but we promise it will be worth it."

CHAPTER 1

WOUNDS—WHY THIS WILL NOT BE EASY

Isn't it funny how infomercials or online ads can totally captivate us?

"This shiny, nonstick, triple-layered pan will change your life!"

"This lightweight skin cream will make you look ten years younger and take away every blemish and wrinkle!"

"This state-of-the-art workout equipment will sculpt your body in just seven minutes a day!"

Sometimes, an ad leaves you thinking, "Huh, I wonder if that product really works?" Then you find yourself searching for it online to read the reviews!

It sure would be nice to take just a few little pills, put on a certain lotion, work out for seven minutes each day, and find yourself looking and feeling great!

Our world seeks the quick fix, the quick hit, the quick high—adrenaline, emotion, dopamine, all of it. We have longings that yearn to be fulfilled, and the world attempts to deliver in the only way it can—by trying to draw us to the latest gadget or fad that claims to satisfy the longings of our hearts.

If there were a quick fix to deal with our fears, insecurities, wounds, brokenness, anxiety, and pains, then someone would have drawn up a formula and made millions on it by now.

While we have all been drawn to many things that claim to bring fulfillment—success, prestige, money, travel, pleasure, fitness, appearance, sex, relationships—deep down we realize that all of these eventually come up short, leaving our hearts longing for a happiness that can seem so elusive.

From our time in Florence, as well as from many years of ministry, we have been blessed to have hundreds of people share their hearts with us— whether it is a college guy who is struggling with a painful breakup; a young adult woman who is questioning her worth because she is twenty-four and has never been asked out on a date; a high schooler who is cutting and suffering because a certain group of students has bullied her since the fifth grade; a father of a teenager who is afraid his child is making all the same mistakes he did at that age; a college girl who is caught between two friend groups and doesn't know what path to take; a grandmother who is desperately trying to instill faith and virtue in her grandchildren; or a young adult man who is questioning what his life is really all about and why it matters.

We could give hundreds of similar examples. You can insert your own unique story and struggles as well; it can be so heavy, and it is never easy— even just to articulate everything going on in our hearts. Ultimately, the pain tends to come down to two key questions:

"Am I enough?"

"Am I truly loved?"

We all have a deep desire to be *seen*, *known*, and *loved*. Our journey through life, though, can get messy, often painfully so. You have probably been hurt—excluded, rejected, and humiliated— which can lead to feeling unloved and unwanted. Whether with words or actions, no one gets out of life unscathed. The marks of these wounds remain for some time, often in ways we do not fully realize.

For example, at one time or another, you have probably been *used* by someone else—either emotionally or physically (or even both).

The experience of being used—and even growing accustomed to being used—leads us to attempt to find ways to cope. Our expectations begin to change. We no longer believe that we will be loved for our own sake, that we will truly have value in someone else's eyes. We learn to adapt, figuring out how to act, what to wear, what to say—all to receive the validation from others we are longing for.

To the men, we want to say we are so sorry for the times you have been hurt, especially when you have been used by the women in your life, emotionally, physically, or probably both. While it's not often talked about, *men feel deeply*. They carry deep within themselves questions such as *"Am I strong enough?" "Am I cared for?" "Am I respected?" "Am I loved?"* We are sorry for the times you have been torn down, belittled, emasculated, and hurt by the women in your life. Those women may never come back and tell you they are sorry, but we want you to know that we are sorry that you have not always been loved in the way you deserve.

We are also sorry for the times you have been hurt by the men in your life, starting perhaps with your own father. While some may have had great fathers, nobody's parents are perfect—the wounds from our fathers (and mothers) are real. And the pain that can come from fathers, brothers, grandfathers, uncles, and male friends is real. We could go on, but you need to know that we hear you; we know your pain, and we are sorry for the times you have not been loved the way you deserve.

To the women, we are so sorry for the times you have been hurt, especially when you have been used by the men in your life, emotionally, physically, or probably both. Women carry deep within themselves the questions *"Am I strong enough?" "Am I cared for?" "Am I respected?" "Am I loved?"* We are sorry for the times you have been torn down, told you are ugly, fat, stupid, or worthless—all the times you have been hurt by men. Those men may never come back and tell you they are sorry, but we want you to know that we are sorry. We are sorry that you have not always been loved the way you deserve, especially by the men in your life.

We are sorry for the times you have not been loved the way you deserve, perhaps by your own father or mother. Sometimes things said—or not said (or seldom said)—leave their mark upon us. This is true not only of parents, but also of other women, since women can be downright cruel to each other. Again, we could go on, but we know your pain—and we are sorry for the times you have not been loved the way you deserve to be loved.

We all have wounds. You are not alone.

This book is about going into the deep places of our hearts, facing what perhaps has haunted us for a long time—and coming out the other side, redeemed and transformed.

It is about wholeness, freedom, and joy. We want to share with you what has been life-changing for so many others—starting with ourselves.

CHAPTER 2

OUR STORIES

One of the questions we get asked a lot is "Did you ever struggle with any of this? Did either of you have to deal with these wounds, insecurities, and fears?"

The answer is most definitely yes! And we still do. We want to be real with you, which is why we want to share our stories with you. The Lord has done amazing things in our lives, but we are still a work in progress.

ANDREW'S STORY

I grew up Catholic, but basically in name only. The Faith did not mean much to me or my family. We went to Mass maybe once a month.

In high school, my life revolved around football, girls, parties, and image.

I went to Benedictine College (where I now teach) for only one reason: to play football. As my freshman year rolled forward, it seemed like I had everything I wanted. I made the team's travel roster, as well as the more limited forty-eight-man playoff roster. I even played in a playoff game as a freshman.

Yet something was missing.

In May, at the end of my freshmen year, our team traveled to Paris to play an exhibition game. At the time, I didn't want to go. I just wanted to go home to train and try to win a starting spot on the team my sophomore year.

But in Paris, my legs were taken out from beneath me in more ways than one: I broke the fibula on my left leg on a kick-off return.

I was devastated; it seemed that everything that made me *me* was gone. So I sank into a depression that summer.

As I returned to campus to begin my sophomore year, I went out to lunch with a professor I had gotten close to the previous spring—Dr. Edward Sri. I'd had him for two theology classes (required of all students), and I was intrigued intellectually. At the time, though, I wasn't ready to change my life. That summer, however, as I sat in my depression, it was like a slow trickle down from my head to my heart. When Dr. Sri and I went out to lunch at the start of my sophomore year, I had lots of questions for him—things that I had been pondering all summer.

As we were talking, Dr. Sri mentioned a course he was teaching that fall called Christian Moral Life. Though the class was already full, he said he would let me take it if I wanted, given my questions. I was already taking seventeen credits that semester, so I asked for a day to get back to him.

Though I had a full class load, I decided to redshirt that season because I didn't want to "waste" a year of football eligibility after not training all summer. So, I went ahead and took Dr. Sri's course—and ended up taking twenty credits that semester!

I do not know how to explain it, but that class changed my life. I walked in thinking it would be about a bunch of "rules"—why the Church says that you cannot do this, you cannot do that—but I could not have been more wrong. Dr. Sri's course was about *freedom, friendship, virtue,* and *happiness.* It soon became clear why I was not happy. I had been made for so much more, yet I was living for so much "less," for things that didn't really matter.

Around this time, I started getting to know a different group of guys. They had a peace, confidence, and stability that I didn't have—something I had never really seen before. My life went up and down depending on how things on the *outside* were going—my play on the field, my performance in the weight room, or other football stats that could raise or lower my status on the team. But these guys had an internal stability and confidence, and it was because they knew Jesus Christ in a living and powerful way.

As I was being drawn more and more into this new way of life, there was still one thing left that I wasn't ready to hand over to the Lord—my relationship with my girlfriend from high school. Good girl though she was, this relationship was definitely not leading either of us toward Christ.

At this time, a residence advisor (RA) reached out to me to teach me how to pray the Rosary. Though I had twelve years of Catholic schooling behind me, he had to correct me on the words of the Hail Mary!

In October of my sophomore year, I vividly remember fumbling through prayers in my dorm room, asking the Lord (in my own clumsy way): "Do you want me to leave my relationship with my girlfriend?" But then I remember saying, almost audibly, "No matter what you say, I'm not going to do it."

I can't explain it, but as I was traveling home for Christmas break that year, I had an undeniable sense of what I had to do. There was no doubt that this relationship with my girlfriend was the last thing holding me back from the life I truly yearned to live. For her sake and for mine, I walked away.

My high school friends could not even begin to understand what had happened to me, and plenty of rumors were going around. I had never felt more alone, and yet more at peace.

By the time I returned to Benedictine for the spring semester, it was hard to shut me up; I had taken my entire athletic mentality and transferred it to what I now saw as the "game of life." The killer instinct I had for training was now devoted in a full-throttled way to my spiritual life. I wanted to go to battle for Christ, starting in my own heart.

Though I kept playing football throughout my four years of college, it was no longer the "god" that it once was for me. Now, football became a metaphor for life rather than my ultimate end.

Sarah and I met the spring after my conversion, when she visited Benedictine. She ended up transferring to Benedictine the following fall, at the start of my junior year.

I look back in thanksgiving for the Lord's providence. I remember when my life was balanced on the edge of a knife—and how terrifying it was when I finally walked away from my old way of life. For about a year, I was able to put my life back together and did not even think about dating. At this time, I was also able to consider the possibility of priesthood, something I couldn't have even fathomed only a short time before.

In these ways, I can see how the Lord was preparing me to meet Sarah. This is a great example of how sometimes a door has to close for a new one to open. Though it can be scary in the moment, I have found that the Lord's plans blow us away when we give ourselves fully over to him. He is never outdone in generosity.

I am now a professor teaching the Faith that I love and am married with six children—I even teach the same Christian Moral Life class that changed my life all those years ago. I have never looked back, and I am so thankful that the Lord so powerfully captured my mind and heart when he did.

SARAH'S STORY

I grew up in a loving, fun, faith-filled Catholic home, with wonderful parents and two younger brothers (who are a foot taller than I am, but I am still their big sister). I am blessed to be close to my family to this day, and I am grateful for each of them in my life. Still, as we have said, no one gets through life completely unscathed.

When I was in sixth grade, my dad battled cancer. The same year, his sister, my Aunt Mary, with whom I was very close, died of cancer at thirty-six. As a bubbly, sensitive, and unassuming little girl, that year rocked me. That was also when a group of girls in my school decided to begin ganging up on me and bullying me relentlessly. At times, I would get physically sick at the thought of going to school, and I ended up switching schools before the end of my seventh-grade year. So I have deep empathy for anyone who is bullied in any way. Of course, my experience occurred long before online bullying—and I shudder to think about how much that would have affected me, had it been available at the time.

My experiences in junior high left me with wounds that I was not really able to name until college. As someone who already struggled with being a bit of a "first-born-perfectionistic-people-pleaser," I spent most of high school making sure that I never felt the pain of rejection or of "not being enough" again. I threw myself into friends, academics, sports, dating, and other "all-American" status symbols, trying to fit in and "make it" by earning people's attention, esteem, and praise.

From the outside, many would have thought: "Oh, she lettered in four sports, she is the class valedictorian, has great friends and a super cute boyfriend, a scholarship to play college basketball—gosh, she really has it all together!" However, the reality behind the walls I had built and the "masks" I wore told a different story: I was an exhausted, empty, confused, and lost young woman. I could talk a big game and I could look the part, but I wouldn't let anyone get too close because then *they might see the truth*—that I didn't have it all together and that I wasn't perfect. Then they would know—*and I would know that they knew*—that I wasn't "enough," certainly not without my self-protective fortresses that I had built up over the years. The crazy thing is the more I leaned on my modes of self-protection, these only made me feel worse on the inside—though I continued to look like I had it together on the outside.

Because of my experience of being bullied, I did not trust women as far as I could throw them. My relationship with men was also complicated; my insecurities led me to seek their attention and approval. It was one of the ways I found my worth.

I had trouble navigating friends and the party scene because I was always thinking more about who I wanted others to think I was than reflecting on who *I* wanted to be.

During my freshman year of college in September of 2001, my entire life fell apart. Two weeks into the school year, 9/11 happened, and I was already terribly homesick. I had a knee injury that ended my basketball season, and my boyfriend of two years cheated on me. To say that my confidence, self-worth, and faith were hanging on by a thread would be an understatement. Many of the things that made me *me* were gone, and my life plans were shattered. The one word that pulls together where I was at that point is *fear*. I was searching, struggling, broken—all the while faking it and earnestly trying to put on my "I'm fine" face.

I once heard someone say that "fine" stands for *freaked out*, *insecure*, *nervous*, and *exhausted*.

Isn't that the truth?! That would have described me perfectly at the time.

Fear had driven so much of my life up to that point, and I see it drive many people today. The four fears I often see are:

- *fear of missing out*
- *fear of being forgotten*
- *fear of rejection*
- *fear of failure*

I transferred to Benedictine College my sophomore year, as an attempt to start over. That fall, a group of female students invited me repeatedly to a retreat at the beginning of the semester. Not wanting to appear rude, but also really wanting them to quit asking, I eventually said yes.

On that retreat, I went to confession to a wonderful priest, and I shared my heart with him—my struggles and my fears. I think it was kind of a last-ditch effort; since I had tried everything else, why not try turning back to God?

That confession changed my life. During it, the priest said: "Sarah, I need you to build a box in your mind and put everything you are struggling with into that box and drop it off at the feet of our Lord. Give it to Someone who can do something about it. Then fall into his arms and let him love you like no human can. You keep looking to people, and especially men, to be your everything and to be your 'god,' but Sarah, they can't be that for you. And you will crush them under the weight of that, and you will always be disappointed. You don't need them to be your Savior because you already have one, so let God be God and let men be men."

It felt as if bricks had fallen off my shoulders. He had articulated how I felt in a way that I could have never put into words at the time.

Then he said to me: "Run to our Lord, fall into his arms, and let him heal you and make you whole. And when you are ready, I want you to run to him and with him; and when the time is right, glance to the side and see who is running *with* you. Who knows, maybe that is who God wants you to be with?"[1]

I remember taking in his words and feeling like I could finally breathe again.

My penance was to sit before the Lord and *ask him who I was.*

I just sat there and kept asking, "Who am I?"

All I could hear was, "You are mine and you are enough."

The wounds of rejection from so long ago were named, and I could see that my ultimate fear was *not being enough for God.* I had kept him at a distance because I didn't want him to truly "see" me, to see that I wasn't the perfect person I tried to present myself as.

That night, my journey back to the Lord truly *began.*

While I would love to tell you that overnight I had it all figured out and that healing was instantaneous, that is not how things usually work. There is no quick fix. But small decisions—small changes, small virtues, small victories, small steps—really do turn into huge results.

This was life changing for me.

You are probably thinking: "So, at what point did you glance over and see Swaff blinking neon green?"

I wish it were that easy; but no—I started running to our Lord, and when I glanced to see who was running beside me, guess who I saw? *A group of amazing Catholic women.*

I thought, "Oh no, Lord, please, anybody but *girls.*" I'd had trust issues with female friends, but these women were different. I was not a chess piece in their game but a sister to them, a sister in need. They changed my life. They introduced me to a whole new group of amazing Catholic men— one of whom would eventually become my best friend, my husband, and the love of my life.

The students in Italy saw the fruit of our transformations that began so many years before. They saw our conviction and commitment; they saw our love for each other and for our children, and they saw the small daily acts of virtue and sacrifice.

Did they also see our not-so-perfect moments? Absolutely!

But it was real. As we lived life with them and listened to their stories and tried to answer their big questions on faith, friendship, dating, vocation, virtue, healing, and all the rest, they saw our *love*—for each other, for them, and for our Lord.

And everything we share in this book comes from that same place of love.

Some things will be hard. But we have witnessed their transformative effects again and again. Sometimes the greatest love is shown when we have the courage to share hard truths, precisely out of a place of love. This is what our students experienced—they knew they weren't being judged, because they knew we loved them.

There are many things in life that are difficult; but these also tend to be the very same things that are most worth our time and effort.

The Christian life is no different.

Challenging?

Yes.

More than worth it—in this life and the next?

Yes, without question.

Do we ever look back with regret about giving our lives totally over to the Lord all those years ago?

Never, not even for a single second. We are so grateful.

CHAPTER 3

WHAT IS ŚRODOWISKO?

Andrew: When I was asked to teach in Florence, I knew exactly what class I would teach—the life of St. John Paul II! Or, as Sarah likes to refer to him, "The Catholic Homecoming King!"

Our students certainly knew who John Paul II was. They had heard of him, and many even held him in high regard. But they did not know his story; they did not know the *man.* I desperately wanted to introduce him to them.

The semester began in Rome and included a visit to Subiaco and Monte Cassino where St. Benedict began his journey as a young man and founded his first monastery. Benedict had left the trappings of the Roman world—its spectacles of entertainment and its numerous temptations—in search of something greater.

As we were leaving on the bus, I grabbed the microphone and drew a few parallels between the life of Benedict and that of our students. Like him, they yearned for something greater than what the world had to offer.

I then referenced their upcoming reading, and I directed them to pay attention to the word *Środowisko* (pronounced "Shro-do-vee-skoh"). I told them that my prayer was that the current semester would become "our own *Środowisko.*"

At that time, they had no idea what this meant, and I left it at that. Over the course of the semester, though, this concept truly took on a life of its own, in our hearts and in the hearts of our students.

WHAT IS *ŚRODOWISKO*?

When Karol Wojtyła (pronounced "Voy-tee-wa," the future John Paul II) was a young priest, after completing his doctorate in Rome, he was sent to St. Florian's in 1949, a parish in the heart of Krakow, Poland, that would become the center of his outreach to university students. In many ways, this experience was where World Youth Day began because it is where his heart for the youth was born.

As Wojtyła's ministry to college students grew, these young people came to refer to themselves as "*Środowisko,*" a Polish word meaning "environment" or "milieu." But it came to mean so much more than any dictionary definition could ever convey.

This period in Poland was incredibly difficult. During World War II, the country had suffered horribly under the Nazi occupation, losing nearly twenty percent of its population—including three million Polish Jews and another three million non-Jews. Approximately one-third of Polish priests were killed by the Nazis, as well as countless religious sisters and lay Catholics.[2]

As Poles sometimes say, World War II is the war they lost "twice." For they went from being invaded and occupied by Nazi Germany only to suffer for decades under the tyranny of communist oppression.

Communism in Poland, as elsewhere, was about far more than an economic system of shared ownership of goods and services. Rather, it was an all-encompassing ideology that included a systematic promulgation of atheism and a sexual ethic that encouraged promiscuity and utilized abortion as a means of birth control. In other words, communism was a belief system directly at odds with the Catholic Church. The ideological struggle was over the dignity of the human person and the truth about human love and human destiny.[3]

Poland's Communist rulers made every effort to sever the nation's culture from its thousand-year Catholic history, seeking to replace it by forcefully instilling atheism in the hearts and minds of Polish youth. In this way, Communism was an official, state-sponsored belief system, one that did not tolerate dissent, especially when it came to Catholics being open about their Faith.

Those who deviated from the state-approved ideology would pay in some way—sometimes violently, sometimes in "softer" ways, such as being publicly ridiculed or excluded from graduate schools or employment opportunities.

While it is not exactly the same, whenever we share this history with young people, they can see the parallels with their own experience today. Some opinions are considered "acceptable" and "correct," while others are not. As in the days of communist Poland, the ideological struggle of today has a lot to do with God—or the *exclusion* of God from public life—and sexual matters.

All of us want to fit in; no one likes feeling like he or she is out of step with the "mainstream." Many fear that if they deviate from the publicly endorsed belief system of the day, they will quickly become marginalized or even "canceled."

The strength of this mainstream ideology, both in Poland under communism and in our own day, is rooted in the profound fear and isolation people feel. When the "mainstream" appears to be so powerful and universal, people can feel as if they are alone—like they are the only ones who have any doubts about the publicly "endorsed" view of things. When people feel like they are alone, they become afraid—and then find themselves quietly conforming to the ideology of the day, making compromises as a way of staying out of trouble.

An image that powerfully evokes what it was (and is) like to live under a communist regime comes from Václav Havel—his famous "greengrocer" parable. Havel was a dissident in communist Czechoslovakia who later became the first president of the post-communist Czech Republic. He offers the following words to capture the experience of living in this constant fear and isolation:

> The manager of a fruit and vegetable shop places in his window, among the onions and carrots, the slogan: "Workers of the World, Unite!" Why does he do it? What is he trying to communicate to the world? Is he genuinely enthusiastic about the idea of unity among the workers of the world? Is his enthusiasm so great that he feels an irrepressible impulse to acquaint the public with his ideals? Has he really given more than a moment's thought to how such a unification might occur and what it would mean?
>
> I think it can safely be assumed that the overwhelming majority of shopkeepers never think about the slogans they put in their windows, nor do they use them to express their real opinions. That poster was delivered to our greengrocer from the enterprise headquarters along with the onions and carrots. *He put them all into the window simply because it has been done that way for years, because everyone does it, and because that is the way it has to be.* If he were to refuse, there could be trouble. He could be reproached for not having the proper "decoration" in his window ... He does it because these things must be done if one is to get along in life. It is one of the thousands of details that guarantee him a relatively tranquil life "in harmony with society," as they say.[4]

This parable captures how communist regimes (then and now) are built on *fear* and *isolation*. And we could insert some contemporary messages or signs many feel compelled to display or endorse today, either physically or online, to demonstrate that they are fully in step with current ideology.

People suffering under communism felt that they were alone, that they were the only ones who felt the way they did. Catholics in such countries felt that they were the only ones who still cared about their Faith. Feeling alone and isolated, they lived in fear. And because they were afraid, they were obedient, feeling forced to accept that such compromises were simply a necessary part of "getting along" in life.[5]

How many of us today find ourselves in a similar situation—at school, at work, or among friends and family? Don't we all feel the temptation to conform to the values and priorities of our time and culture?

There is a part of all of us—even if only a small part—that desperately wants to be in step with the elites of our day. It is natural to want to be in step with what the well-spoken, educated, and popular people think. Aren't we sometimes exhausted by feeling like we are always on the defensive?

This is what living in communist Poland was like. And it has clear parallels in our country today.

If you have ever seen black-and-white pictures of Karol Wojtyła as a young priest, celebrating Mass on an overturned kayak used as an altar, with oars tied together in the form of a cross—this is *Środowisko*! To escape the communist oppression of the city, Wojtyła began taking these young people on trips to the mountains—camping, kayaking, and skiing. When you see pictures of him shaving in the woods, cooking over a campfire, smiling and laughing with groups of young people—these are glimpses of the *Środowisko* family. These are examples of him rallying young people who didn't want to conform to the communist "orthodoxy" of the day.

Communist officials were particularly vigilant in squashing Catholic youth groups for fear that young people would be influenced in a way contrary to the ideological goals of the regime. Then, as now, this was an intense battle over the hearts and minds of the youth, over what future society would look like and what it would value. When Wojtyła went on these excursions, he had to go "undercover," since the communist officials would not allow a priest to be out and about with young people.[6] So he did not dress as a priest, and the students called him *wujek* (pronounced "voo-yek"), meaning "uncle."

Środowisko became an "environment" of true freedom and authenticity for these young people, where they could experience real fellowship and communion with one another. It was a zone of freedom where they could fully be themselves—where they were free to express their faith and build friendships animated and infused by their faith, where they could ask questions and openly pursue their deepest convictions together. As one *Środowisko* member later described, "We could live more freely because we were free inside."[7]

Members of these groups describe Wojtyła in incredible ways. They say they could talk to him about *anything*; nothing was off the table. As one said, "He had mastered the art of listening."[8]

Alongside this familiarity and intimacy, it was clear that Wojtyła and these young people weren't just "hanging out"; they were gathering for a purpose. This was a group that was going somewhere; they were living life on mission.

Wojtyła loved these young people enough to speak the hard truths with them, especially things they needed to hear as young adults. He was both loving and challenging—even demanding. They respected him and looked up to him, and they wanted to follow where he was going. As one *Środowisko* member later put it, "Today, many priests try to be like the kids. *We were trying to be like him.*"[9]

This was exactly what these young people needed, as they were trying to navigate life in the midst of an all-encompassing atheistic regime. They needed someone who loved them and understood them, but who also had the conviction and courage to speak the truth.

St. John Paul II later described his experience with *Środowisko* as an act of *accompaniment*, and it became his distinctive pastoral approach throughout his life. He accompanied these young people on their journey—he listened to them, loved them, and came to understand them deeply. He loved them so much that he couldn't let them settle for easy answers; he encouraged them to go out into the deep—to the very heights and depths of who they could be in Christ. Then as now, navigating sex, dating, and love was a challenge for these young people, especially with the prevailing state-enforced ideology of the time.

It was here at St. Florian's, in John Paul II's own words, that he "*learned to love human love.*"[10] He believed in young people and in their capacity for greatness. Even when their attempts at authentic love fell short, he was convinced that "in the depths of their hearts, they still desire a beautiful and pure love."[11]

The *Środowisko* community grew into the hundreds, and they would continue to stay in touch throughout their lives. These friendships—which included several marriages that came out of this group—became lifelong.

For twenty-five years, from 1953 until he was elected to the papacy in 1978, Wojtyła and this group went on a two-week kayaking trip every August. Even after he became pope, they continued to stay in touch. As the years went by, the children of this original group of young people began to accompany their parents on these trips. By the end of his pontificate, John Paul II even got to know many of their grandchildren as well.

What happened in Florence with our students was not only a matter of learning about the life and teachings of St. John Paul II—our students fell in love with *Środowisko*. They loved learning about these young people who, like St. Benedict, went against the grain. They admired these young Polish students, who were so much like themselves and who faced very similar challenges as they do today. Our students wanted to imitate their intentionality in gathering for a purpose. They, too, wanted their faith to become the unifying center of their friendships—resulting in a whole new depth to their friendships (and dating relationships), something they could not have imagined before the trip.

We consider it a tremendous honor and blessing to have shared in this adventure with them, to have accompanied them in this way. We were even able to take them to one of our favorite places to lead pilgrimages—to Poland—where we were able to relive John Paul II's story on-site, along with those of St. Maximilian Kolbe and St. Faustina.

That semester in Florence became our own *"Środowisko,"* as we grew incredibly close to those students and remain so to this day.

Our group of forty-eight students were not all close friends prior to the trip—in fact, many of them didn't even know each other. But they forged friendships that will last a lifetime.

Like the original *Środowisko*, we have already had three marriages come out of that semester—and none of the couples were even dating when we left for Italy!

When John Paul II later reflected on his most formative influences, he always pointed to his experience with *Środowisko*. While he helped form these students deeply in the Catholic Faith, in many ways they also formed him. The same is true of our time in Florence. We were privileged and blessed to accompany our students at such a pivotal point in their journey, but they also formed us in powerful ways.

For all these reasons, *Środowisko* means so much more than any dictionary definition could ever communicate. *Środowisko* refers to a community gathered for a purpose; it refers to friendship that is anchored by a common pursuit of a transcendent good. It means friendship enhanced and illumined by the light of faith, walking together with mission and purpose, and supporting one another along the way. And it means having a great time together—full of fun, laughter, and a contagious joy.

The concept of *Środowisko* helped our students break the chains of fear and isolation, giving them the courage to follow Christ without fear, even when this means going against the grain.

Our prayer is that this book will, in some way, become a shared *Środowisko* with you.

Life is never easy and is always a bit messy. But living with meaning and purpose, with the support of friends journeying alongside you, can make all the difference.

We pray that *Środowisko* can offer light and strength, amidst times of darkness and confusion, especially when you feel afraid and alone.

You are not alone.

We are excited to walk alongside you.

PART II

WHAT IS GIFT AND GRIT?

CHAPTER 4

WHERE DO WE FIND MEANING?

While it would be fun to jump right into a practical discussion on friendship, dating, and our walk with the Lord (*OK, how many of you have already peeked at the "Can Men and Women Be Friends" chapter!?*), these next few chapters lay important foundations for the more practical material to come.

For starters, an important question to ask is this: What is a stable foundation upon which we can build our lives—a foundation solid enough to give us meaning and purpose throughout the entirety of our lives?

If we build the meaning of our lives upon sand, then we will find ourselves grasping at illusions of happiness, chasing things that seem to satisfy for a time but fall short in the end.

Deep and authentic *meaning* grounds our lives as *gift*—so we can in turn become a gift for others; without this in place our relationships suffer, with one another and with the Lord.

These next two chapters undergird the life of *Środowisko*, forming the bedrock of our efforts to live the Christian life with peace, purpose, joy, and confidence, especially in the face of opposing ideological forces.

The mind is a powerful thing—our deepest convictions dramatically affect how we live, especially when it comes to our peace and joy. Later, we will see that the payoff comes in developing and applying these fundamental convictions.

What are you convicted of? What are you committed to?

Our convictions and commitments determine a lot about where our life is going and how we live it out, and they become a tremendous source of strength when times are tough.

MEANING AND GIFT

It has been said that the most common cause of depression is not lack of self-esteem but lack of meaning in one's life. When we lack meaning, we lack purpose—and then we lose hope.

Today, a great many people, both young and old alike, have simply lost their story. They have lost the overarching narrative that gives reason and purpose to their lives.

They have lost meaning.

For so many today, the grand narrative of their lives looks something like this: excel in sports and in school (so they can get into the "right" college, in the event that sports don't work out as a profession), find a job, buy a car and a house, go on vacation every year, and eventually retire with a winter home someplace warm.

Many also feel the pressure to stay in shape and look their best, worshipping at the altar of the mirror, in hopes of looking great at the pool, gym, or that one week at the beach.

In addition, our social media presence must be up to par. Often, it is not so much about experiencing a given moment but the need to capture it with a photo or video so we can post about it later and demonstrate to others how wonderful our life is going, or at least have it appear that way. The pressure mounts to look the part in person *and* on the screen.

This entire process continues year after year, with the dynamics of junior high repeating themselves again and again at different stages of life in different ways—and yet much the same.

And we wonder why we are so full of anxiety and restlessness! We can end up bitter, depressed, agitated, angry, unfulfilled, and bored with life.

Can this be all there is? Is this all that our life amounts to?

Deep down, we know there must be something more, but we just don't know where to turn. Where can we find genuine and lasting *meaning*?

For so many today, life is like a story with no plot. It seems as if we must come up with our own "meaning" as we try to find something—*anything*—to become passionate about and devote our lives to. Otherwise, how else will we numb the drudgery and apparent emptiness of our existence?

While "you do you" and "do whatever makes you happy" might be modern battle cries, they don't fix the problem. The reason for today's sadness and loss of meaning is that we know deep down that "self-made meaning" is *no meaning at all.*[12] Real meaning must be *received.* It can't be something that merely comes out of my own self-projection, or my own attempts to manipulate people or projects in order to make my life feel more important.

Real meaning must be anchored in the *truth.* In a culture that embraces nothing beyond "your truth" and "my truth," the shifting sands of this relativism prevent us from finding any real footing, any real meaning and purpose to our lives.

This is the dilemma of our time.

GOD AND MEANING
Many today have not so much rejected God; they are just preoccupied by all the energy it takes to "make it" and "look the part."

Instead of gazing at the stars in wonder, our vision tends to be entirely focused on the things of earth. As Jesus suggested in the parable of the sower, for many, God's word in our hearts is "choked" by "the cares of the world" (see Mark 4:7, 18–19). Our relentless effort to make it in the eyes of the world drowns out our thirst for something more.

Add in a little screen time to fill any dull or unpleasant moments, and whatever chance we might have of God's presence taking root in our hearts is quickly suffocated. The "oxygen" of the spiritual life is simply taken up by other things.

The result is an inescapable sense that our hearts are weighed down by anxiety, restlessness, and a deep sense of unfulfillment and even boredom.

It is not that screens or social media are evil. It is just that *busyness*—a mainstay of our culture—has a distinct way of choking out any real, abiding meaning and joy from our lives. If our "leftover" time is taken up by mindless scrolling, then we have a perfect recipe for missing out on the true and genuine meaning of our lives.

Being overly busy (with all our spare moments going to screen time) tends to make us live superficial lives without genuine joy, peace, and gratitude. It is hard to be grateful when all we can think about is getting through the next task at hand. How often do we say:

"I'll be happy if and when _____."

"If only I can get through _____, then life will finally begin."

"If only I can achieve _____."

In the end, our accomplishments and goals are never enough—never enough in our own hearts and never enough when we constantly compare ourselves to others. For we tend to compare our "behind the scenes" with everyone else's "highlight reel," making us so focused on what others have that we cannot see the good in our own lives.

If our lives come from the hand of a loving Creator, then our lives are a *gift*, a gift full of meaning and purpose. We are here for a reason. We have a mission in God's plan, a part to play in the greater story. Indeed, we are here "for such a time as this" (see Esther 4:14).[13]

Such *received* meaning is rooted in the ultimate source of reality. Nothing can give life a more secure anchor than this, and nothing can offset the angst of modernity more than recognizing that we are not alone; we are here for a reason.

We are not alone, nor are we the ultimate masters of our destiny.

While we might like to be fully in control of our lives, the thirst for radical autonomy and independence comes at a price—the price of *being truly alone and having nowhere else to turn but to ourselves.*

Deep within our hearts, we long to receive the true meaning of our lives—from the God who truly directs the script of our lives, who loves us and has a plan for us.

In truth, we don't want to just *ad lib*—we want to play the role we have been given in this great play by the divine director. Each of us wants to fulfill a role appointed *just for us.* We want a mission and purpose that we didn't create all by ourselves.

We want to be seen, known, and loved.

We want to matter to someone other than ourselves.

We want our lives to mean something beyond merely *our* own goals and ambitions.

When each of us embraces the received meaning of our lives from the hand of our Creator, we come to see ourselves as part of a much greater story. We discover that we have a part to play in this great story—and, mysteriously, a part that will be left unfulfilled if we do not answer the Lord's call for us.

What could make our lives more meaningful and exciting?

If we ignore this calling, our hearts will be left unfulfilled. Each of us longs for something far greater than anything our goals and ambitions could ever satisfy.

This is exactly what Frodo in *The Lord of the Rings* came to understand from Gandalf, as he lamented being entangled in the drama of the ring:

"I wish it need not have happened in my time."

"So do all who live to see such times," Gandalf famously responds. "*But that is not for them to decide. All we have to decide is what to do with the time that is given to us.*"[14]

Gandalf's words point to a fundamental truth: our time has been *given* to us—as a gift and a calling. We receive it from the hand of God himself; it is not merely of our own making. Like Frodo in *The Lord of the Rings*, we have an immensely important role to play in this great story.

It is not an accident that you are where you are. God is writing your story, and you are writing it with him.

The mystery of God's mission for each of our lives unfolds over time.

Living life with an eager discernment of this mission unveils the abounding meaning of our true purpose. Our personal walk with the Lord and our embrace of his mission for our lives will have a lasting impact well beyond the horizon of our own lifetime, even unto eternity.

CHAPTER 5

WHAT IF MEANING ALONE IS NOT ENOUGH?

One of the things we often hear from young adults is that they deeply want to make an impact; they want to change the world. They want to leave a legacy.

These are admirable desires, and they are steps toward genuine meaning—which gives rise to hope, purpose, and a sense of mission.

But *meaning alone is not enough*—not if we are serious about making a true and lasting impact.

There is a second component, which is essential—namely, *grit*. Without grit, our meaningful hopes never get past the raw enthusiasm about things we would like to do or be someday. This desire alone is not enough to bring them about.

Think back to Sarah's story in chapter two, when she spoke about her conversion during confession. She described how this experience led to "*small* decisions—small changes, small virtues, small victories, and small steps," which then turned into "*huge*" results.

When we only think about meaning, we tend to limit our thoughts to *big* things. We can forget that *big changes* and *heroic people* are formed when we commit to being champions in the *little* things. Grit is what enables us to take the little things seriously—those intermediate steps that make greatness possible.

WHAT IS GRIT?

"Grit" is typically defined with reference to "sand" or "gravel." That is, it is something *hard*. This fundamental meaning leads to certain connotations with respect to the human person, which is how we are using the word. Here, grit means a "firmness of mind or spirit: unyielding courage in the face of hardship."

Life always presents us with challenges. We will fall on hard times; our dreams will hit road bumps, and suddenly, these dreams may not look as rosy as they once did. We may even feel duped or lied to and wonder why we ever set out on such a path in the first place.

What will carry us through in these moments of struggle?

This is where grit comes into play.

In some ways, grit aligns closely with the virtue of *patience*, which is considered a part of courage. There are two aspects of courage: the first *confronts evil* (for example, the courage of a soldier); the second *perseveres* through an evil that cannot be removed (as in the courage of a martyr).[15] Patience is an essential part of the latter aspect of courage, which enables us to persevere through difficulty while maintaining our peace of mind, serenity, and even a deep and abiding joy.

NOT JUST "WHEN THE LIGHTS ARE ON"

Some people have this type of perseverance and work ethic "when the lights are on"—that is, when others are watching and their reputation is at stake.

Andrew: This was definitely true of me before my conversion. I would spend countless hours in the gym, running or training in various ways. At the time, I claimed this was for football, but it was really the "altar of the mirror" that drove me to such excruciating heights, as I sought to satisfy my own vanity.

Did I have this kind of work ethic to rake the leaves or wash the dishes—or do anything else that seemed "beneath me," especially if it didn't serve my own glory? Not a chance!

Like me, many who have a solid work ethic in certain areas of life can crumble when faced with trials, especially when they find themselves no longer in the spotlight and their enthusiasm begins to wane.

This can happen in every area of life. *Sarah:* I can vividly recall what a challenge motherhood was early on. I had two little boys, fourteen months apart, both under two years old. While this was a beautiful and special time, the total dependence of our little guys upon us—and the seeming loss of freedom this entailed—was eye-opening. I certainly came face-to-face with my own selfishness, pride, and vanity.

Something similar can happen when the excitement of a new job tapers off. We might feel like we are not making the impact we thought we would. As a result, we can find ourselves disenchanted and disillusioned—perhaps even tempted to leave the job after only a short time.

This can also happen in ministry, when we feel like our talents are being underutilized, or when the initial luster begins to wear off and the experience of monotony sets in.

And the same dynamic can play out in relationships or even marriage.

There will be many times in life when we don't feel like we are our team's "most valuable player"—when we feel undervalued and underappreciated—and we feel like what we are doing doesn't really matter. This can be especially true for young moms or dads, whose unconditional love for their children seldom receives the praise or attention it deserves.

What will carry us through during these seasons?

Things that really last—things that are worth having and pursuing—aren't built in a day. Real virtue grows when it is tested; character matures through trial.

This is where grit—sustained courage, patience, and perseverance—is crucial to persevering in a life of virtue. It is crucial to sustain a *meaningful* life.

While it is easy to get excited about the *idea* of virtue, it is much harder to see it through to the end. But this is precisely what separates the "men and women" from the "boys and girls."

Many can seek virtue when it is *seen, noticed, respected,* and *admired.* It is another thing altogether when the scene changes—when virtue starts to *cost* something.

As C.S. Lewis put it, even Pontius Pilate "was merciful—*until it became risky.*"[16]

The difference between heroic virtue and mere enthusiasm lies in the *grit of sustained commitment.* This is the difference between a work ethic that performs when the "lights are on," and one that is steadfast and accountable when nobody is watching.

This is the difference between someone we can count on through thick and thin, as opposed to someone who proves unreliable when things get hard and it is no longer "all about them."

FROM MEANING TO GRIT—AND TRUE FREEDOM
When we lose our sense of meaning, even the mundane challenges of life cripple us.

Whereas, *meaning gives rise to hope*—which empowers grit and gives us motivation to continue through trial. When the monotonous and mundane are infused with meaning and purpose, we can find the strength to carry on, with sustained perseverance, patience, and even joy.

This is the stuff of virtue, as any athlete knows. Many get excited about being great, but they don't have the grit to put in the work when no one is watching. The same is true for musicians, actors, scholars, and countless other areas of life, where excellence comes only through consistent effort over time.

Here *discipline equals freedom*.[17]

We often think of freedom as simply the ability to do whatever we want, whenever we want. But true freedom is the *ability to do the good*, and this freedom grows over time and with practice, as is the case with the following examples:

- Learning to play a musical instrument

- Learning a foreign language

- Mastering any athletic skill that is at first clumsy and awkward, but over time and with practice becomes more and more fluid and effortless

- Getting in shape, enabling one to run longer and harder—with less pain, the better shape one is in

Any basketball player can make a lucky shot. But a good player is consistent and reliable. He or she is "free" to play the game with excellence and to do so consistently, due to years of training. The fruit of such training and discipline results in a stable skillset, making us *freer* to play at a higher level, and with greater consistency.

This person can be relied upon.

The first time we perform an athletic task or try to get in shape, it is usually clumsy, awkward, and even painful. But with practice, we become better at the skill; over time, we get in better shape. The same is true of learning a foreign language or a musical instrument—the more we practice, the better we get. We then achieve a greater freedom to perform at a higher level, joyfully and on command. The better we are at something, the more joy we take in performing that activity, and the more consistent we become.[18]

Our growth in virtue follows the same path. It is not just about performing an isolated virtuous act. It is about *becoming the kind of person who has interiorized a particular virtue*, making it a stable part of who we are—a "second nature." We "play" how we "practice," and this is true not only on the field, but even more so in life.[19]

The practice of grit forms our character. Every time we don't buckle when adversity strikes, we become more adept at not buckling in the future. As we undergo trials and push through them without letting adversity paralyze us, we become more skilled at facing difficulties.

While *meaning* catapults us on our path, giving us purpose and mission, *grit* is necessary to sustain us on this path. Meaning gives us our divine mission; grit fuels us to stay the course and finish the race.

HAPPINESS AND DESIRE

Virtue leads to authentic happiness. This is not a superficial happiness or a mere subjective contentment. The happiness that flows from virtue is more like how we feel after a great workout—very different from how we feel after eating our favorite dessert.[20]

While cookie dough is great (ask any Swafford!), it satisfies only for a time and eventually leaves us hungry for more, and for something different. The same is true of the temporary satisfaction that may come from looking at ourselves in the mirror, from achieving status, or from social media—this "satisfaction" lasts only for a time and always leaves us yearning for more. We are like the Samaritan woman at the well, searching for water that truly quenches—and yet we return to the superficial waters of the world again and again, only to find ourselves parched and thirsting for more (see John 4:1–30).[21]

Our hunger for acceptance and prestige is a sign of our deeper hunger to be *seen, known,* and *loved*—especially by the God who created us and loves us and has a plan for us.

Ultimately, our happiness and fulfillment will only come from fulfilling the mission to which the Lord has called us, especially in and through our relationships.

SUPERNATURAL GRIT

We shouldn't view grit merely in secular terms. For the world, "grit" refers to hard-nosed perseverance and persistence.[22] While this can go a long way, it does not fully encompass what we mean.

Grit informed by faith—*supernatural grit*—is not just a stoic resignation to get through hardship or difficulties. Such resignation only goes so far; we might be able to "get through" something but only begrudgingly, often with interior resentment and bitterness. This does not rise to the full level of virtue—since *how* we bear a difficulty matters a great deal.

For instance, it is not enough just to be "nice," say to a roommate or family member. We have all known people who are occasionally "nice" on the outside while secretly "keeping score" on the inside, often harboring internally how their "kindness" has now placed us in their debt. These same people can be quite skilled at finding subtle ways of making known just how "nice" they have been to us lately.

Most likely, we have all been on both sides of this dysfunction at one time or another.

Therefore, it is not just about our actions. Rather, *how* we go about things is intrinsic to our growth in virtue (or lack thereof). True virtue requires more than just an outward action; it does not "keep score" or leave such a gap between our actions and what is happening on the inside.

A person who is truly virtuous experiences *joy* when performing a virtuous act.

For this reason, supernatural grit doesn't just get through difficulties begrudgingly. *Supernatural grit empowers us to see difficulties as mysteriously coming from the hand of God*—as gifts, though often very different from the "gifts" we would have chosen for ourselves.

In this way, supernatural grit doesn't just *get through* difficulties—it offers them back to God as gifts in return, as a holy sacrifice.

True supernatural grit does not fall prey to bitterness or discouragement but keeps us from becoming overly distraught when things don't go our way. It enables us to steadfastly see all things in light of faith, in light of eternity.

For there is always a story being written that is bigger than what we can see. Supernatural grit helps us live with this reality in mind.

In the end, grit (especially supernatural grit), is necessary for the formation of virtue—and therefore necessary to attain authentic happiness and fulfill our relationships.

HOPE AND SORROW

Some ancient Christian writers describe sorrow as a deadly sin. They are not referring to the emotion of sadness—and certainly not to clinical depression. What they mean by sorrow is an *irrational sadness that loses sight of eternity.*[23]

Here, supernatural grit is the direct antidote to this kind of sorrow.

People with supernatural grit do not lose hope; nor do they lose their sense of peace and joy, precisely because they know they never bear their trials alone—and that their trials are *never without meaning* in God's eyes, no matter how annoying, insignificant, or despairing they might seem.

The combination of this deep meaning—received by God as gift—and supernatural grit is what makes a saint; it is what makes for heroic virtue. It is what enables us to get through the less-than-glamorous challenges we will inevitably face—and to do so with peace and joy. Not only does this combination make a saint, it's also what makes the best of teammates, bosses, coworkers, friends, and spouses; it is what makes a person someone we really want to be around.

REAL LIFE IS NEVER "ELSEWHERE"

The confidence that meaning and grit bring does not stem from a naive or superficial sentiment that "things will get better" or that "everything will eventually turn out for the best." The source of our confidence lies deeper, in the knowledge that in all things, great and small, we have a purpose and a mission—even in our toil and sufferings. This can be difficult. But even if things don't get better, we find our mission and purpose amid the *concrete circumstances* in which the Lord has placed us.

We are certainly not referring to situations of abuse, from which we should remove ourselves as quickly as possible. Apart from these grave situations, there is a real sense that the mission of our lives is never *elsewhere*, a temptation we will feel strongly when frustration sets in. When times get hard, it is easy to think that if only we were somewhere else—in a different job or home or state in life—then we would flourish; then we would fulfill our potential and be truly happy. Such illusions tend to be the Devil's playground, causing us to jump from one thing to the next, never realizing that setting down roots is often the true path to authentic growth and happiness.

There may well be situations which, with proper discernment, we should change. But the point here, which St. Ignatius of Loyola especially emphasizes, is that the time of desolation (a spiritual down time, when we feel far from the Lord) is not the time of sober decision-making—it is the time when we are most prone to the Evil One's deception.[24] We should be leery of our default inclination to change course the moment things get hard, and we should be aware of this spiritual dynamic. Perhaps most importantly, our discernment needs to mesh with the objective realities of our life and vocation (e.g., the moral law and the solemn vows of marriage or priestly ordination). If we allow the subjective to reign supreme (especially during times of desolation), we will lose the objective anchor of our lives and soon find ourselves aimlessly following our fleeting desires.

Instead of resenting our current circumstances (which indeed might be burdensome and frustrating), supernatural grit helps us to see them in light of faith and embrace them as the post to which the Lord has currently stationed us. Instead of asking "why?" in a hopeless and despairing way, supernatural grit asks the Lord, "*What do you have for me here?*"

All of us can probably think of times when we succumbed to this temptation and failed to be faithful to the task of the present moment. *Andrew:* I had just begun my graduate work in Old Testament and Semitic languages. While I loved learning Hebrew and Aramaic, I remember thinking about all the other things I also wanted to study (e.g., philosophy, philosophy of science, history, literature, among others), all the things I didn't have time for. This "wandering" of my mind and heart became a distraction, taking me away from the work to which the Lord had called me at that time.

Sarah: As I have mentioned, while I loved being a new mom, it was a big change. The early years of marriage, young children, and graduate school meant sacrifice. It meant we couldn't do a lot of things we wanted to. Even important things that were staples for us in college and were key to our growth in faith and virtue were not as easy to come by with little ones. The many sacrifices involved took a great deal of grit to carry out, especially when trying to do so without losing our peace and joy.

When we come to resent our circumstances, we experience the fierce temptation to believe that real life is somehow eluding us, making us feel trapped and enslaved by our concrete circumstances. It's so easy to start thinking, "*I'll be happy if ...*" or "*I'll be happy when ...*"

Often, our frustration is due to unrealized expectations, especially when we find things more difficult—and less exciting—than we had anticipated. But pushing through here makes all the difference. *It is a matter of being faithful to what the Lord has given us in the present moment.*

Rather than resenting our circumstances, supernatural grit enables us to see our circumstances as gifts from the Lord—gifts to be embraced and returned to him with love and devotion.

This is not easy because these gifts are often not what we would have chosen for ourselves. But this is exactly what heroic virtue is all about. What matters here is not success but *faithfulness.*

Such faithfulness, especially in the little things, can change the history of every age. It is the wheel upon which salvation history turns, from the apostles to the present day.

Heroic virtue and faithfulness, with peace and joy in the midst of trials, dramatically affects the experience of those around us, especially those in our own household. This is why John Paul II so frequently said, "Civilization passes by way of the family."[25]

After all, don't you want to be around a person of supernatural grit, someone who doesn't wallow in self-pity or take their frustration out on you when things don't go their way—someone who joyfully sacrifices for you and is able to continue through adversity with peace and joy?

Wouldn't you want this kind of person in your life? Wouldn't you want such a person as a spouse or friend?

If you answered yes to these questions, then it only makes sense to strive to become this type of person ourselves. And becoming this kind of person starts with conviction and commitment—since we won't get very far without a strong sense of meaning and grit.

When these convictions take deep root within us and we commit to them in the little things, life is never the same.

In truth, embracing both deep meaning as a gift from the Lord and supernatural grit are the foundations of what Środowisko is all about. As we have seen in our own lives and in the lives of others, they are the deepest foundations upon which to build authentic and lasting friendships and relationships

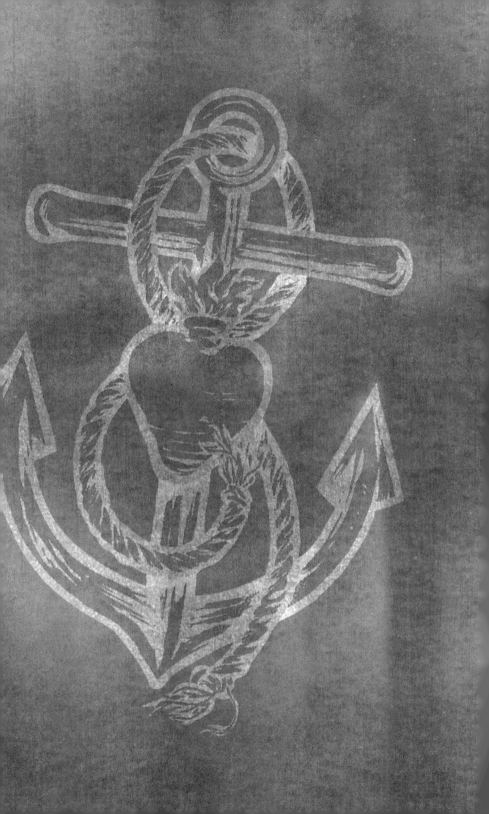

PART III

LIVING GIFT AND GRIT IN FRIENDSHIPS

CHAPTER 6

HOW DO I NAVIGATE NEW AND OLD FRIENDSHIPS?

"You become like the five people closest to you—choose wisely."

We ran across this quote years ago, and its truth becomes clearer with each passing year.

Whether we realize it or not, more is *caught* than is *taught*. In various ways, we tend to imitate those around us, especially those who form our inner circle.

One student we spent a lot of time with had a big heart and a great love for the Lord. For much of his college years, though, he struggled with being *consistent*. He would have periods of being on fire for Christ and then fall back into old habits of drunkenness and sex. He desperately wanted affirmation from all sides—from his Christ-centered friends and from those he partied with. Sometimes he would seek out a "middle position," being drawn toward those who seemed to be Christ-centered but who also wanted to fit in with the party crowd.

This young man continued to struggle with this tug-of-war on his heart. He wanted to follow Christ and go "all in" as a disciple. But he could never quite muster the strength to do so consistently, always finding himself pulled in competing directions. Looking back, he describes how this resulted in a deep sadness—feeling chained down—because he never felt completely free to be the person he truly wanted to be.

Like this student, we might sometimes feel torn between the person we long to be and the direction certain friends are pulling us. While these friendships may have been strong in the past, if we find ourselves drawn to a deeper conversion in Christ, our relationship with them can undergo a certain strain.

A sign that our friendships are changing is when conversations tend to revolve around the past, for example, stories about things we did together. This may involve certain activities that we are now trying to remove from our lives, such as drunkenness, sex, pornography, or drugs. We might have the poignant sense that if we didn't talk about "life in the past"—or if partying together ceased—the friendship would soon end.

Though this may be hard to hear, a friendship that is stuck in the past is a *dying* friendship because there is no longer an ongoing relationship in the present. This is true even if both of you have all the goodwill in the world toward each other. The reality is you may be growing apart, to the point where you no longer have that much in common—except your shared past.

WHAT IS FRIENDSHIP?

What we are about to write can be challenging, but it is liberating. Think back to what we presented earlier, especially with regard to meaning, grit, and *Środowisko*. If these are to become realities in your life, you will need to foster friendships built on these foundations. We gravitate toward becoming like our closest friends. If we want to live a life built upon these foundations, then how we view friendship may need to change.

True friends see the same good and cherish the same truths. They have a shared vision for life, which is what unites them, as they accompany each other toward this common goal—just as a team is united in its pursuit of victory.

In this sense, *a friendship is as deep as the good that binds the two together*, as deep as the good they both hold dear. It is all about the depth of what we truly have in common.

If all we have in common is sports, then that is as deep as our friendship goes; if all we have in common is working out, having the same place of employment, or going to the same school, the same is true here. If all we have in common is enjoying the same activities—whether drinking or drugs on the one hand, or playing cards, golf, or shopping on the other— then that is the depth of our friendship. If we remove the activities that we do together, then these friendships tend to quickly fade—unless there is something more to them.

There are different kinds of friendships because we are joined with others in different ways, by different kinds of "goods." While this is normal, it is worth reflecting on exactly what binds our various relationships together, in the present not just the past.

So, the question for all of us is: *What is the good that binds me and my friends together?* How deep is it? How stable and abiding is it? Do we share the most important and fundamental things in common? Or are we only united by more superficial goods and actually go our separate ways when it comes to what matters most?

It is not that we need to drop our old friends, "ghost" them, or become standoffish. Nonetheless, it is true that the people we choose to run with, those we confide in and with whom we spend the bulk of our time, will eventually shape who we are.

WHY WE NEED GOOD FRIENDS

Our most important friends become "workout partners" in the game of life. We want to surround ourselves with people who love us enough to call us to greatness; we want close friends who desire the same goal as we do—*and desire it as earnestly as we do.*

Both of us have athletic backgrounds. We know what the life of an athlete entails and what real training means. A good training partner is one who has the same goal as we do and desires it with the same tenacity. When this is not the case, frustration and resentment soon follow. A workout partner with substandard goals—or substandard motivation and commitment—is not the workout partner we want or need.

The same is true of friendship. We need friends who love us as we are *but too much to leave us that way*. We want friends with whom we can be real and vulnerable but who also love us enough to hold us accountable and call us to greatness—friends who love us enough to speak the hard truths into our lives, especially when we need to hear them most.

If we are serious about the goal—a life of authentic virtue and Christian discipleship—then we need to cultivate friendships with those who desire this same goal, and desire it as ardently as we do. Such deep bonds of friendship are formed not by running "at each other," but by running toward the same goal together.

True friends are those who help nurture the good habits we are trying to form in our lives. True friends are people we look up to and want to imitate. They become instrumental in living the Christian life because they help form and shape who we are and who we are becoming.

BEING TRUE TO WHO WE ARE

Toxic friends, in contrast, are those who work against the good habits we are trying to form. They pull us away from the person we are trying to become. They might try to make us feel guilty for not doing certain activities with them (e.g., drunkenness, drugs, sex). They may downplay our conversion, as if it were merely a phase—one they may consider too radical, as they try to "rein us back in."

Andrew: When I was in the thick of my conversion, I had roommates at the time who saw my budding conversion exactly in this vein. It took a good bit of time for them to realize and accept the fact that Christ was becoming a permanent fixture in my life.

We need to be fully honest with our friends about the depth of our encounter with Jesus. We need to have the courage to be ourselves by making the importance of our faith known to them. We can do this without being "showy" or "in your face" about it. We need only to have the courage to be our true selves. After all, no one can argue with our testimony, our personal encounter with the Lord and what he has done in our lives.

If a friendship is going to continue, we cannot be fake and dishonest with our friends.

Andrew: Some of my toughest battles after my conversion came from being around old friends from high school. For example, when an inappropriate joke or comment was made, early on I had the temptation of falling back on nervous laughter—not knowing what to do or what to say, and not having the courage to express even the slightest disapproval at what was said. I was fake, and I was afraid to be myself around them. *Sarah:* I also struggled with family and friends in this way. Not wanting to seem too "radical," I would shy away from conversations or anything that might seem controversial.

There is no need to start arguments or expect old friends to become saints overnight. But it is important that we have the courage to be ourselves. A powerful way to do this in tough and uncomfortable situations is to find quick, witty ways to express disapproval, without being provocative or confrontational. *Andrew:* For example, after my conversion, when someone on the football team would use the Lord's name in vain, I would say with a smirk, "He loves you." They knew what I meant, and it became a running joke, as they would grin back at me. It was a small way for me to express disapproval at their language, without being antagonistic or overly prudish. Out of respect for me, they would usually avoid using such language when I was around.

Only if our old friends come to respect and acknowledge the change and permanence of our conversion can a genuine friendship continue. If they do not respect us enough to acknowledge our conversion—and not to seek to undo it—then there is not much of a friendship to speak of.

HOW IMPORTANT IS THIS, REALLY?

In our experience, when all is said and done, the clearest indicator of whether a person's conversion to Christ is likely to stick often comes down to whether they begin to prioritize Christ-centered friendships over old friends who are pulling them in a different direction.

For this reason, the people we choose to live with is pivotal.

Sarah: My decision to transfer to Benedictine—and to give my new female friends a chance—led to me living in a suite with eight amazing women. Throughout the course of that year, those women helped me grow and heal in a whole new way.

Andrew: The same was true for me when I was going through my conversion. I chose to live with my new Christ-centered friends during my final two years of college. In some ways, these new roommates weren't natural fits—none of them were football players, for example. But I knew that the men I chose to live with were going to form me in a deep way, even without my realizing it. I wanted roommates who wanted to help me become the man I truly wanted to be, not those who would subtly (or not so subtly) push me in the opposite direction.

Looking back, this choice to live with friends who encouraged us in our moral and spiritual lives was decisive for enabling our conversions not only to stick but to take off and thrive.

WHAT DO I DO WITH OLD FRIENDSHIPS?

This is hard, but we have to be honest with ourselves on this issue.

It is easy to become the "mom" or "dad" of the group, always trying to keep our friends out of trouble. It is easy to think that our witness will eventually draw our friends out of a life of hard partying. Though well-intentioned, it generally doesn't work out this way.

In college, there was a time after our conversions when we desperately wanted to evangelize friends and acquaintances who were enmeshed in the party culture. For a few months, we went to various parties with the intention of evangelizing and drawing them out of this environment.

While this effort bore some fruit, often our presence was taken as an implicit endorsement of what was happening at these parties. In other words, we had become the moral barometer for many of these friends. *Andrew:* I knew many guys on the football team, stemming from our countless hours together at practice, weights, meetings, and team travel. And Sarah was the social butterfly then that she is now.

Our friends at these parties were always ecstatic to see us. Upon our entrance, they would shout, "Swafford is here!" And they would even chant Sarah's name. But the overall impact of our presence at these events led to the attitude of those there that, "If Swaff and Sarah are here, then what we're doing can't be *that* bad." After all, they knew that if what was happening was really that problematic, we wouldn't be there.

Rather than drawing our friends out of the party scene, our attendance at these parties made them feel more comfortable where they were. It really didn't move the needle toward conversion or bring about a change in their lifestyle.

When a conversion stirs in our heart, we often want our old friends to have the same experience. This is a beautiful sentiment. Sometimes the Lord's work in our life sparks interest in theirs. But often, we are met with indifference, or even outright defiance and resistance.

It was far more effective for us to find "neutral" places to hang out with old friends. For example, we would hang out at their house, grab lunch together, or play a game of pickup basketball. The key was finding ways to affirm them and connect with them in neutral environments, when they were not engaged in things like binge drinking, drugs, or sex.

Seeing them in these neutral situations tended to bring about more meaningful conversations, which also gave added clarity as to where these friendships were going—whether they were likely to continue in the future or if they were already beginning to fade.

HOW DO I EVANGELIZE MY OLD FRIENDS?

Ironically, the best way to evangelize old friends is to foster our Christ-centered friendships. As we grow in a community full of life and on fire for Jesus (i.e., *Środowisko*), we can slowly invite our old friends into these groups. The more our old friends see the change in us *and in our new social circle*, the more compelling our witness becomes. Such a community shows our old friends that we're not "weird"—and that they won't be at a loss for friendship and community if they join us.

In fact, they may well have a better time than they are now—it just might look different.

In college, we used to do all kinds of "alternative" things, such as "cosmic bowling" (think bowling, plus blacklit dance party). We would gather our Catholic friends, and then we would intentionally reach out to others. *Andrew:* I would invite a few football buddies, and Sarah would invite some of the women she had met. Typically, we had a competitive wager on the line. Most often, it was guys against girls and the loser had to pay for breakfast afterward, usually well after midnight. We would all be laughing, talking, having a blast together.

Often, those who came out with us would say things like: "This has been the best time I've had all semester. It's the first time anyone has really talked to me and asked me about my life and how I was doing—*and actually meant it.*" These friends and acquaintances noticed how different this experience was in comparison to the typical party scene they were used to. With us, they were valued as persons, not simply as objects for another's gratification. On these outings, they got a taste of deeper friendship and authentic community. Many of those who experienced conversions within our extended friend group later confided that only after going out with us did they cease numbing their pain and distracting themselves from the emptiness and meaninglessness they felt in life.

One current student described her experience of *Środowisko*-type parties this way: "They aren't any different than other parties; it's just that no one is drunk, and no one is sneaking upstairs for something sexual—and the conversations are deeper."

In our experience, the key to evangelization is the combination of "*normal*" but *different*." In college, we encountered a group of friends who seemed "normal"—we could connect with them; we had similarities. But they were also very "different" from anybody we had ever known. Their lives beat to a different drum; they answered to the Holy Spirit rather than the ruling winds of the world. Before encountering Christ, our lives went up and down with sports, image, etc. But these new friends had an interior joy, peace, and confidence that we had never known. They were *different*—and they weren't afraid to be different. Yet, they were also so "normal"—which built a bridge from us to them, from our old lives to the new.

Both aspects—normal but different—are essential. Without the *difference* of Christ's complete lordship over our lives, there is no incentive to dramatically change one's life. This difference made us want what they had—and that is what drew us in.

The same is true of our cosmic bowling and similar efforts (e.g., concerts, fireside chats, dinners, swing dances, and other "alternative" hangouts). Those who went out with us knew we were different. They saw that no one was getting wasted, and we only drank alcohol if everyone was twenty-one. This is exactly why they were so mesmerized by how "normal" we all were—by *how much fun we had together*.

Many were surprised at how much fun we had without the crutch of excessive drinking or focus on sex appeal, so prevalent in the typical party scene. They saw authentic human living, conversation, and friendship taking place without "masks," without the games they were used to. And this difference drew many of them in, as it did for our students in Florence.

Środowisko—friendships anchored in the good and running toward Christ together—is a powerful way for us to grow toward becoming the people we long to be. But the witness of such communities is also very often *the most effective way to reach our old friends* and share with them the beauty and power of the new life we have found in Christ.

CHAPTER 7

I KNOW GOOD FRIENDS ARE CRUCIAL, BUT *HOW* DO I MAKE THEM?

After speaking, one of our favorite things to do is to meet people and talk with them one-on-one. Whether we are speaking to young adults or adults, men or women, in America or on another continent, we hear the same thing: "Thank you for your talk. I really got a lot out of it, but *I have no one to live this out with.* I have a few good friends, but I could never talk with them about my faith. I know I need good faithful friends, but *where do I find them and how do I make them?*"

During childhood, meeting people can come about somewhat easily. Growing up we likely had classmates or teammates (or neighbors)—people in our lives at the same age or stage as we were, who just happened to be around.

For some people, these acquaintances may have blossomed into deep friendships. Others "knew" lots of people and yet found themselves lonely—like they never had a real friend in the world.

Even those who had lots of friends and acquaintances may never have found a set of virtuous friends, peers who shared their deepest values and priorities, especially when it comes to faith.

LIVING ON MISSION

It can be hard to pin down exactly what it means to live with deep meaning, but the phrase we often use to capture it is *"living on mission."* By living on mission, we mean living with a clear sense of purpose and intentionality, journeying toward an explicit goal—ultimately union with Jesus Christ in this life and the next. This is exactly what *Środowisko* is all about.

This plays directly into our question about how to form the friendships we are all looking for. In truth, the best way to form and foster deep and lasting friendships—and to grow in virtue and holiness—is to *live on mission*.

Again and again, we have seen that when people live this way, they soon find themselves surrounded by others who want the same thing. The reason so many find strong faith-based friendships in college is because, often for the first time, they find themselves in a community of people sincerely *living on mission*. We see this all the time at Benedictine, as well as at other universities with a strong Catholic identity and presence. It can also happen at a parish. All that is needed is a few people who want to do this together with an urgency that fuels one another. The fact is, *conviction* is *contagious*.

If we want to foster deep Catholic friendships, we need to live on mission ourselves and find others to run with.

In the years right after college, we cannot rely solely on specific programs or groups. For instance, you might have access to a dynamic Catholic young adult community, but maybe not. You might have access to great Bible study groups at your parish, but maybe not.

In the end, we need to be creative. We cannot rely on programs to set things up for us. *Sometimes we just need to be the program ourselves.* While this isn't easy, with a bit of nerve and creativity we can make this happen.

To start out, you don't need a lot of people. Just find a few who are as committed as you are and begin to live on mission together and see what happens. Often, what starts out small catches fire and in a short while becomes a thriving community, forming deep friendships.

The reason this is so important is because even well-established Catholic communities can sometimes lose their sense of mission over time. Sometimes, just a few people sincerely living on mission together can form a deeper, more thriving Catholic community than one that has become stagnant (or maybe even cliquish) and lost its tangible sense of mission and purpose.

The key to the community living on mission is that the community does not see itself as the ultimate goal. Rather, the goal of the community is to be united in journeying together toward Jesus Christ. When a community becomes the end in itself, it loses its sense of mission and begins to collapse in on itself.

Virtuous friendship is always *about* something—virtuous friends are united in their pursuit of a goal. They are *journeying* together on *mission*. And the deeper their sense of mission, the deeper their friendship. The same is true for a community as a whole.

BE OPEN TO GOD SURPRISING YOU

One issue we often see at this point in the search for peers who are living on mission is that we are sometimes too quick to judge by appearances. In our experience, as we lived more and more thoroughly on mission, we found ourselves becoming good friends with people we probably would not have envisioned ourselves hanging out with earlier in life. On the surface, it might have seemed like we didn't have much in common. But in Christ, we were united by something so much deeper that surface differences didn't matter nearly as much.

The apostles witness to this. They are sometimes described as twelve "fishermen," but this is actually incorrect. Only four are explicitly described as fishermen—Peter, Andrew, James, and John. The "other" Simon (not Simon Peter) is called a "zealot"—a member of one of the factions that sought to take up arms and violently revolt against Rome.

Matthew was a tax collector, which at the time was a Jew who benefitted
monetarily by working with and for the hated Romans who were
oppressing his own people. The individual apostles clearly had different
personalities, gifts, backstories, and passions. On the surface, there is
no way that Simon the zealot and Matthew the tax collector should be
hanging out at all! But their union in Christ and their shared apostolic
mission overcame these differences.

Even if we have some virtuous friends with whom we click, we have to
be open to the ways God might be nudging us. For example, we want to
be inclusive, inviting others in and allowing our group to expand as the
Lord wills. It might be that the virtuous friendships we need most are not
the ones to which we were immediately drawn. Sometimes people with
a different background can challenge us to grow in ways that might not
happen otherwise.

DON'T FORGET THE HEART

Another pitfall that people serious about living on mission sometimes
fall into is that—while they are attentive to the objective aspects of a
faith-filled, virtuous friendship—they can neglect the importance of the
human element, such as the importance of bonding at the emotional
level. They may forget that it is OK—even important and essential—to
have fun together.

In other words, we have seen people "overdo it" in their attempts to
form deep Catholic friendships—as if the only legitimate subject of
conversation should be deep theology or one's devotional life. So much
focus can be placed on the objective goal and mission that people end up
neglecting the deeply *human* aspects of friendship.

In practice, what this means is that, in addition to praying and seeking the
Lord together, we need to *share life* with one another. We need to laugh
and cry together; we need to have fun together.

The things that secular culture values in friendship—trust, security, being
yourself—are taken up in a virtuous friendship. As Aristotle said long

ago, virtuous friendship is "complete" friendship.[26] Virtuous friendship includes what is present in more superficial levels of friendship (for example, having a good time together) and takes them deeper.

Therefore, the deepest friendships are not only built upon the solid foundation of living on mission and journeying together toward a common goal, they also take on a *shared mind and heart*, rejoicing in each other's triumphs and sharing in each other's sorrows. A virtuous Christian friendship connects on all levels:

- *spiritually—moving toward a common goal in Christ*
- *emotionally—becoming one mind and heart*
- *having fun together—e.g., enjoying common activities*

This deep union of mind and heart is illustrated in an experience most of us have had at one time or another in telling a friend a story in our life. Sometimes, we experience disappointment when it feels as if he or she is not really listening to what we are sharing. They might frequently interrupt us, saying things like, "Oh yeah, that's just like the time *[fill in the blank]* happened to me."

On other occasions, though, our friend seems to *feel* the story with us. We do not even need to explain the ins and outs of how we felt because he or she has truly entered our emotional orbit. Our friend is not thinking about himself or herself; they are *feeling* the story with us. This is what it means to become one heart and mind.

SELFLESSNESS IS MAGNETIC

One of your friends probably came to mind when we were talking about someone *feeling* a story with us. Similarly, you may have thought of another friend who tends to interrupt your stories to talk about himself or herself. In some ways, the difference between the two comes down to real humility, which is the virtue that helps us forget ourselves and truly enter the world of others.

Contrary to popular misconception, humility is *not* about having a low opinion of ourselves. Rather, the virtue of humility enables us to take our eyes off ourselves and turn outward in love of God and neighbor. In other words, it is about self-forgetfulness, helping us to no longer be preoccupied with ourselves (whether in our talents or our weaknesses). As C.S. Lewis is famously paraphrased: *humility is not thinking less of ourselves, but thinking of ourselves less.*[27]

In our experience, making good friends is not so much about being "in the know" as it is just being the kind of person who takes an interest in the lives of others. Most people, once they feel comfortable with us, like to talk about themselves and are usually quite moved when we show an interest in them.

People want to *matter* to someone else. They want to be known and loved. And a powerful way of loving them is simply to ask them questions about their life.

The selfless person is like a magnet; people are drawn to them. When we live on mission and become the kind of people who ask questions and take an interest in other people's lives, we will not be at a loss for deep and meaningful friendships. If we are willing to be creative in bringing people together, this recipe definitely works. We are speaking from years of experience—we have seen this happen again and again.

PRACTICALLY SPEAKING, HOW DO I FOSTER SUCH FRIENDSHIPS?

Making and fostering good friendships does not come about without effort. Even among good people, friendship is not simply "automatic."

We get this. And we hear from many people (especially men) that they would like a step-by-step process of how to go about it, since making friends is not easy—especially today.

Even very good people, with a shared vision of life and shared goals, don't necessarily become great friends overnight. We have to facilitate this progression.

So, here are four basic steps to forming deep and lasting friendships:

1) Begin by attending events or joining groups, such as a Bible study, service project, mission trip, or a Catholic young adult event, conference, or retreat. These are gatherings for an intentional purpose rather than just to "hang out." Introduce yourself, especially if you have seen someone more than once at one of these events. It is so important and valuable just to know someone's name, especially when we learn it from them firsthand.

2) Once you have met someone and know their name, be sure to say "hello" when you see them. After a few encounters, ask them how they are doing and find out more about them—for example, where they are from, what they do, their hobbies, etc. One of our favorite questions to ask is: "So, what keeps you busy?" This gives people a chance to mention a whole host of things—family, work, hobbies, etc., which then gives you a great many things to ask about later on as a follow-up.

3) Find ways to spend time together. This may start out by simply doing things together (e.g., sports, getting lunch in a group, shopping, etc.). A friendship—even within a like-minded community—doesn't necessarily become super deep right away (and if it does, it may be artificial). Typically, friendship in such a community begins with respect and goodwill and simply having a good time together.

At this point, invite the person you have met and begun getting to know somewhere with your other like-minded friends. Before you depart and go your separate ways, make sure you have exchanged contact information (if you haven't already).

In the coming weeks, while you should not act as if you are best friends over text or messaging, don't drop off the face of the earth either. Eventually, invite your new friend to do something again. While we might fear the vulnerability and spontaneity of back-and-forth, face-to-face interactions, especially with someone new, it is essential to get together in person for an authentic friendship to develop.

In fact, prioritizing face-to-face, in person encounters is important for another reason: when we resort exclusively to texts or messaging, we often stay within our comfort zone and fail to branch out to new people. In doing so, we may be missing out on great friendships that may be right around the corner. We may also be inadvertently depriving others of their chance for deeper friendship.

Sarah: After a talk I gave to young adults, a young man approached me. He mentioned that he had been part of the Catholic young adult community for several years. He said that his group used to gather regularly after Mass and touch base on a place to go, usually meeting up at a nearby restaurant. At a certain point, the group stopped gathering after Mass. He then discovered that the rest of the group were now messaging each other electronically—and he had somehow been left off this chain of communication. He expressed sadness at no longer feeling like he was part of the group—without having any way to break back into it.

Though his exclusion could have been intentional, it was probably just an oversight. While the "planners" of the group likely did not consider him a centerpiece of their community, this doesn't mean they necessarily sought to exclude him. They just weren't concerned enough to make the effort to include him—and this indifference became more pronounced when they began to make plans electronically.

This is a valuable lesson. We do not know who we are leaving out—who might be literally within ten feet of us—when we only communicate electronically. Face-to-face, we can physically see the person and their body language that says they would like to join us. Conversely, communicating solely electronically can make it easy to act as if they don't even exist— which is what happened to this young man (and many others who have shared similar stories with us).

4) After a while, friends need to bring up their deeper goals for friendship (though this doesn't need to be super formal). In other words, friends will want to avoid *just* having a good time together and never taking things further. Verbalizing what each hopes for in the friendship in terms of

living on mission together is a gigantic step toward it becoming a truly virtuous friendship.

In a virtuous friendship, we desire above all the *objective good of the other*—that is, we want our friends to reach their ultimate goal, union with Christ in this life and the next. If we truly love our friend, we can never say, for example, "If that is what makes you happy, then I support you," if their actions are contrary to their ultimate end. Rather, a virtuous friend might say, "You be you—*provided your actions are informed by faith and virtue.*"

Real happiness comes only by way of pursuing the good, by way of virtue. For this reason, each virtuous friend loves the other enough to challenge them and speak the hard truths with love. This is expected from both parties because they have both acknowledged their shared desire for this kind of friendship. But it's very difficult to get to this point if there hasn't been some explicit acknowledgment of what a virtuous friendship is and what it entails and a mutually expressed desire for this kind of friendship.

So, to recap, the progression of a virtuous friendship looks like this:

1. Introduce yourself and learn the other person's name.

2. Ask how he or she is doing and make "small talk" by asking some basic questions (e.g., "Where are you from?" "What do you like to do?" "What keeps you busy?")

3. Spend time together, doing common activities and getting to know each other better.

4. Make an effort to verbalize your deeper goals for friendship beyond just "hanging out." Be explicit about your common understanding of what a virtuous friendship is and what it entails.

Once the process begins, *spending time together* is the crucial element. A true friendship takes time to develop if it is to be authentic and lasting. (There is a reason why we are suspicious of a "pseudo-familiarity" that comes on too strong, too fast, as we suspect it may be only skin-deep and disingenuous.)

As parents, we have come to dislike the phrase *"quality time."* We have found that true *quality time* only comes about through an extended *quantity of time.* That is, if you shoot the breeze long enough and do things together, eventually breakthrough conversations occur. Especially with our kids, we can't manufacture these moments from scratch; they only tend to happen when we have been hanging out together for a significant amount of time. Both in parenting and fostering friendship—there is just no substitute for really sharing life together, and this means prioritizing time spent together.

OK, I HAVE SOME GOOD FRIENDS, BUT WHAT IS THE NEXT STEP?

We love to talk about the three essential—though sometimes challenging— ingredients that make for a virtuous friendship: *availability, vulnerability,* and *accountability.*

Availability. As we have emphasized, friends must make spending time together a priority. One of the greatest gifts you can give someone is your attention. Phone down. The gift of your eyeballs—focused, listening, caring—*available.*

Virtuous friends need to be in each other's lives, even if they are geographically distant. This means doing things such as "checking in," knowing what is going on—the ups and downs of the other person's life. Friendship is a skill and a virtue because it takes time and effort to do it well. Many otherwise wonderful people don't have solid, virtuous friendships because they have failed to make time for them.

Sarah: When I was speaking in Australia, a group of young adults told me about their "Wednesday Nights Out." They would go to dinner and would place all their phones face down in the middle of the table to allow them to be undistracted and available to each other. Whoever reached for his or her phone first had to pay the bill! Genius! Now that is *availability in action!*

Vulnerability. As we become more and more comfortable with each other, we begin to share our hearts with one another. We become one heart and mind. Vulnerability is about entering into a place of freedom and security with our friends, where we can be our true selves—acknowledging our honest weaknesses and struggles, our fears and hopes, our highs and lows. Here, we allow our friends to love us as we are, even as they encourage us to become the people we are called to be in Christ.

Accountability. This is the most difficult but the most powerful ingredient for virtuous friendship. The above two build connection; they build rapport and a foundation of trust between friends. This connection, however, needs a firm anchor in truth; it needs to be rooted in a shared vision of the meaning and purpose of life. Life is a journey toward a *goal*, which is why it has *meaning*. As great "workout partners" in the game of life, virtuous friends love each other enough to hold each other accountable.

In the end, *sin makes us sad*. So it is not loving to encourage a friend on a path of sin. Truly virtuous friends call each other to greatness and are not afraid to do so. A virtuous friend *empowers* the other for a life of virtue, instead of *enabling* them in their sin.

Many of us have few friends (if any) who are willing to speak hard truths into our lives, who have the guts to tell us what we need to hear but do not want to hear. We should be grateful for their courage. Sometimes, such tough conversations become the necessary precondition for us to break out of something that has us chained down and is keeping us back from becoming all that God has called us to be.

Step four above makes accountability easier to live out. Friends who have previously expressed their desire for this kind of friendship and have discussed their common understanding of what a virtuous friendship entails understand that accountability is to be expected. This provides a natural and organic framework of love and respect in which to have difficult conversations when they become necessary. They are not a "surprise," coming out of nowhere—and they don't come across as judgmental because we have given the other person permission to hold us accountable. While this doesn't make accountability easy, it can make it much less awkward and jarring.

DEVELOP A GAME PLAN

By "game plan" here, we mean creatively coming up with structures that invite and facilitate the kinds of conversations described above. This can be simple and informal. Perhaps it is having a weekly lunch or check-in to follow up on how you both are progressing on various goals—for example, prayer or growth in a particular virtue. This provides a safe space where we can be vulnerable and receive regular support and be held accountable. (In fact, just knowing that there will be a weekly check-in is already built-in accountability.)

An amazing group of guys committed to this in a profound way. They shared with us that each of them was struggling with purity, but they had enacted a plan that was really helping. If any of them had committed a sexual sin, they would text each of the other guys. From that moment on, all of them fasted for the *next twenty-four hours* and prayed for each other. This was a powerful experience of mutual solidarity and support. Just knowing that you would have to text or make that phone call—and knowing what your actions were going to put your friends through— was a powerful deterrent from sinning sexually. While these men were not perfect, their brotherhood was strengthened tremendously by being available, vulnerable, and accountable to one another.

Nearly all of them went on to be groomsmen in each other's weddings, and we can only imagine what their brotherhood meant to their brides!

Are these friendships easy to form? Do they happen by accident or overnight?

No.

But are they worth the effort and investment of your time and energy? Are they nothing short of life changing and pivotal in our efforts to become the person we long to be?

Absolutely.

OK, let's take everything that's been said up to this point and dive into the next chapter, which asks, "*Can men and women be friends?*"

CHAPTER 8

CAN MEN AND WOMEN BE FRIENDS?

"But why would you want to get to know a girl if you don't want to have sex with her?"

Sarah: I remember my eyebrows going up as I looked at the freshman guy, standing with a group of his friends, who had just said this to me. I was dumbfounded, but not really shocked by his question. (I was not shocked because this is so common in the college "hookup" culture.)

So, *"Can* men and women be friends?"

And, "Why would men and women want to be *just* friends?"

Unfortunately, like the freshman guy quoted above, many men and women see male-female friendships as simply *a means to an end.* They often see these relationships either as potential "friends with benefits" or just a necessary step in the process of pursuing their next boyfriend or girlfriend.

Some men, for example, have confided in us that they have a "standby" list containing the names of women with whom they have developed a friendship, all of whom are "potentials" for dating (or sometimes just "hooking up").

Women often have their own versions of the "standby" list, with guys waiting in the wings who are ready and willing to fill their emotional "love tank"—male friends who provide the attention they would otherwise receive from a significant other, but without the commitment or strings attached.

Both men and women can be adept at using each other, physically or emotionally, and often both at the same time. They might not even fully understand that this is happening or even recognize this as using each other.

As a response to this situation, one may get the impression from some Christians that men and women need to stay completely separate until they are ready to talk about courting and marriage. While this is an exaggeration, it does represent one extreme approach to the question about whether men and women can be friends. Ironically, there is an underlying agreement between this extreme reaction and the guy's comment above, in that both imply that genuine friendship between the sexes is not possible.

Others claim that this question is a nonissue because, in their view, men and women are basically the same, with no real difference between the two.

The best answer lies somewhere in between. Men and women are not the exact same, and yet they *can* be friends.

Not only can they be friends, but such friendships are also essential for growing in virtue. It is wonderful when men and women can engage in healthy friendships, in environments of trust where we can view each other as persons with dignity, not simply as potential romantic or sexual partners. Our culture makes such friendships difficult but not impossible—and they are worth fighting for.

We cannot tell you how powerful it was for both of us to have healthy friendships with the opposite sex after our conversions. *Sarah:* It was incredible for me to be friends with men as brothers in Christ and not as potential dating partners or affirmation "pieces." It was wonderful to

CAN MEN AND WOMEN BE FRIENDS?   87

value each other as *persons*, without ulterior motives. I didn't want to be an obstacle to their virtue or holiness. I respected them and wanted to help, not hurt, them.

It was something that neither of us had ever really experienced before, and it was pivotal for our growth in virtue, friendship, and faith. It helped us grow in our ability to love—sincerely seeking the good of the other. We learned to value others for their own sake, not merely for what they can do for us. We learned how to love authentically and not use one another, even unintentionally.

Nonetheless, friendships between men and women tend to take on a different character than friendships with those of the same sex—precisely because men and women *do* have important differences. For this reason, while male-female friendships are important for our growth, they can also have certain distinctive pitfalls.

WHAT DOES IT MEAN TO BE HUMAN?

Men and women share a common humanity, a common human nature; in that sense, far more unites us than divides us.

Aristotle classically defines human beings as "rational animals."[28] The reference here to "animal" means we have bodies with sensory powers of perception and bodily desires and emotions. "Rational" refers to more than just being clever and having the ability to problem-solve—it means having the capacity to wonder, think abstractly, use language in grammatical ways, make laws, recount history, and ponder philosophical and scientific issues. Our rationality enables us to distinguish between *appearance* and *reality*, between *what we see* and *how things actually are*. For this reason, our rational nature makes us unique within the animal kingdom.

Being a "rational *animal*" means we are *embodied* persons, who have been endowed with an intellect and will that yearn for the infinite—while simultaneously experiencing bodily desires for food, drink, and sex, as well as fears, hopes, and sorrows. Our body is a constitutive and essential aspect

of who and what we are, as a *union* of body and soul, made in the image
and likeness of God (see CCC 365).

Men and women share this *common human nature.* Both sexes have desires
and emotions, stemming from our common bodily nature (which are
informed by our rational and spiritual nature). Practically speaking, this
means that, contrary to popular belief, *men are not just sexual robots, with
no feelings* and *women are not just bundles of emotions, with no sexual desires.*

For this reason, ministry to men needs to address the heart, in addition to
sexual temptation. And ministry to women, which usually tends to focus
on the heart, also needs to address women's sexual struggles.

HOW ARE MEN AND WOMEN DIFFERENT?

While more unites us than divides us, there are still clear differences in
tendency between men and women. Here, we can draw on St. John Paul II's
distinction between "sensuality" and "sentimentality." *Sensuality* refers
to physical attraction and desire, while *sentimentality* refers to emotional
attraction and desire.[29]

Sensuality tends to be stronger and more immediate in men, whereas
sentimentality tends to be stronger in women. In fact, many women say
that their experience of sentimentality (i.e., emotional attraction) greatly
affects their experience of sensual desire.

Though playing on a stereotype, there is some truth to the notion that the
way to woo a woman has a lot to do with how she is made to *feel*—what
kinds of things are said to her, and whether she feels like her emotional
needs and desires are being met and anticipated. In contrast, the visual
appearance of a woman can be enough to grab a man's attention, regardless
of his emotional attachment to her.

While there are exceptions, our experience and that of many others
suggests that this distinction in tendency points to something real and
worth paying attention to. Consider, for example, the often-repeated
observation that *men will use love to get sex* and *women will use sex to get
love.* It is so easy for men and women to use each other to get what each

wants in the moment, whether physical, emotional, or both. And the differences between men and women are often manipulated precisely in this way, in order to facilitate mutual use of one another.

Over the years, guys have explained to us how this plays out in today's "hookup" culture. A guy typically finds a girl at a party and starts up a conversation. As the night goes on, he seeks to use the right words to push the woman's emotional buttons. As he warms her up to him emotionally, he prepares her heart for a sexual encounter with him later that night. While this young lady might be physically attracted to the young man, the strength of her attraction is likely increased a great deal because of how he made her feel throughout the night.

Another way these differences show up is at the physiological level. Not to be too graphic, but it is a biological reality that the sexual arousal curve for men and women is different. This is why St. John Paul II has written that a man needs to exercise discipline in becoming an unselfish lover when it comes to marital intimacy.[30] For this reason, "foreplay" for the woman is often an all-day affair, long before the marital embrace in the bedroom—meaning that her arousal in the bedroom is often greatly impacted by the emotional connection (or lack thereof) she has felt with her husband throughout the day. In this regard, women are like Crockpots and men are more like microwaves.

Even when women struggle with sexual sins (mistakenly thought to be only a male issue), this can still play out differently. A woman we know who ministers frequently to women with pornography addiction believes that this is often rooted in wounds these women have from their relationship with their father or a brother, especially in terms of their experience of rejection and abandonment. She believes the sexual struggles of such women are a way of coping with these unmet desires for love and acceptance.

This may not be true of all women who struggle with sexual sin. But it does point to the fact that even when the issue is the same on the surface, differences between men and women may still be at play underneath.

Here, what looks like an erotic addiction for these women may not be just about physical pleasure, but a desire for emotional love and acceptance. This makes sense in light of John Paul II's teaching that sentimentality tends to be stronger in women.

Of course, this is not to say that a man couldn't struggle in a similar way (seeking erotic content out of an unmet emotional need and desire for love and acceptance); nor is it to say that a woman's struggle with pornography and masturbation couldn't ever be primarily about lust and physical pleasure.

Men and women both experience sentimentality (emotional desires) and sensuality (physical desires). But the former tends to have a stronger pull in women, while the latter exhibits greater immediacy in men.

These differences in tendency between men and women are strong enough to mean that friendships between men and women are likely to have their own distinctive dynamics—sometimes even being perceived differently by each sex.

For example, one study found that *men are quicker to view their female friends as potential romantic partners.* Men who are attracted to a female friend tend to *overestimate* how much their female counterparts share this attraction. At the same time, according to this study, women tend to *underestimate* the romantic attraction their male friends feel toward them, since these women assume their own lack of romantic interest is reciprocated.[31]

None of this should keep us from seeking healthy male-female friendships. But we need to be aware that these friendships have distinct dynamics and challenges—precisely because men and women are in fact different. Since these friendships are important and worth fighting for, the question is: How can we avoid their distinctive pitfalls and live out these friendships in a virtuous way?

LIVING ON MISSION WITH
FRIENDS OF THE OPPOSITE SEX

As we have seen, the best way to form and foster deep friendships is to live on mission and find people to live on mission with.

The same is true for friendships between men and women.

When groups of male friends join with groups of female friends on mission, journeying toward Jesus Christ, this is an explosive combination. It is very powerful for men to be built up by women, and for women to be built up by men, in transparent and virtuous ways.

The most important thing that curbs the common pitfalls in male-female friendships is for a group to have a clear sense of mission and purpose. When a group takes on the character of a virtuous friendship—that is, when the group's center of gravity is intentionally *about* something, i.e., growing closer to Christ—this acts as a powerful check on the impulse to seek friendships with the opposite sex for selfish motives.

This mission-oriented environment and ethos of the group helps give rise to authentic affirmation of the opposite sex. Because of their commitment to pursuing the good together, men and women become less prone to befriending each other solely to find their next "significant other" or to use each other emotionally or physically.

To be affirmed authentically by the opposite sex in friendship for its own sake—not for some ulterior motive—is an extremely powerful and formative experience; it certainly was for us after our conversions.

And the same was true for many of our students in Florence. *Andrew:* Not only were they able to experience this with one another, but many later acknowledged that it was pivotal for them to see how I interacted with the female students and how Sarah interacted with the male students. Several students admitted later that they had never before experienced friendship with the opposite sex *for its own sake* (and not for some ulterior motive). They watched our comfort and confidence in who we were around the opposite sex (what living on mission looked like in action), and it became a model for them.

When men and women gather together on mission, running toward Jesus, they grow immensely in their encounter with one another. They learn to love one another—in the sense of sincerely willing each other's good—instead of playing games with each other's hearts. Growing in real friendship with the opposite sex—grounded in faith, virtue, and authentic love—is exactly what *Środowisko* is all about. It is an experience of love, the very opposite of using.[32]

A PARADOXICAL SIDE EFFECT OF MEN AND WOMEN LIVING ON MISSION

While not their intent, these groups of men and women journeying together with a clear faith-filled purpose often result in wonderful dating relationships and even marriages. But this is a side effect, not the purpose, of such a group. We do not pursue virtuous friendship just to find a spouse. And yet this is what often happens when men and women are running together toward our Lord. We know this well from personal experience, both in our own lives and in ministry. As we mentioned, three marriages came out of our time in Florence, and none of these couples were dating at the time!

It is a bit of an ironic paradox: A group of virtuous men and women gathered together, living with a clear sense of Christ-centered mission, *is* the best place to find the spouse you're looking for. *But this cannot be one's reason for joining such a group.* Unfortunately, this often happens in Catholic young adult circles, where it becomes clear that some are not really interested in friendship; they're just looking for a spouse.

A good relationship is sort of like authentic happiness: It doesn't happen when we go around "looking for it" at all costs. It comes about when we sincerely pursue the good. It is the fruit of a virtuous life. Similarly, great dating relationships tend not to happen when we are desperately looking for them. Rather, they often come about best by "accident," as the side effect of pursuing the good wholeheartedly alongside others who are doing the same.

COUNSEL FOR MARRIED AND RELIGIOUS (AND SINGLES) IN MALE-FEMALE FRIENDSHIPS

Sarah: On several occasions, I have been asked to write a version of *Emotional Virtue* for married couples or religious (i.e., priests, religious sisters, or monks). In all honesty, though, one simply needs to apply the same principles in the book to whatever state of life one is in. We have watched these dynamics play out over the years, and it's clear that the same principles are essential and relevant in any vocation.

When we settle into our vocation, this creates a context in which there is less worry about miscommunication or mixed signals. Still, the need for caution remains, as the same dynamics of male-female friendships described above can show up here, though in slightly different ways.

Importantly, it is not wrong to find yourself attracted to someone—whether in personality or appearance. We are innately attracted to the true, good, and beautiful. The key, however, is what we *do* with that attraction and how we handle it.

If we are attracted to a friend or colleague, we should be wary of certain dispositions we might experience and be honest about the internal movements of our hearts, asking ourselves things like:

- *Are we looking for an excuse to "bump into" this person? Do we try to find an excuse to text or call them?*

- *Are we thinking of this person excessively when they are not around? Do we encourage such thoughts in our hearts?*

- *Do we find ourselves looking at their social media for no apparent reason?*

When affairs and scandals occur, they might seem to happen almost by "accident." But the truth is that they often stem from a failure to be attentive to the earlier movements of our hearts.

The key to fidelity is to recognize that *we are more in control of what grows in our hearts than we realize*. While attraction is spontaneous—and not a problem in itself—the previous examples point to how indulging an attraction in our hearts encourages it and makes it grow. At this point, the attraction becomes intentional, because we have been negligent in taking custody over our hearts. In contrast, we can starve inappropriate thoughts or desires, which will eventually make them subside, weaken, or even die. At a minimum, this can be done by *not* falling into the pitfalls mentioned above—i.e., by not "manufacturing" reasons to bump into or communicate with this person unnecessarily, by not encouraging our thoughts about this person, and *especially* by not perusing their social media.

It is a mistake to think that falling in love is something totally irresistible. Rather, we *let* ourselves fall in love with someone we're not supposed to be in love with. We have the choice to either give in and encourage this growth in our hearts or to "starve" it. The choice to be faithful begins and ends right here.

We are blessed to have many priests and religious sisters as our dear friends, and we have known a good number of seminarians over the years. Simply because someone professes religious vows does not mean that he or she ceases to be a human being with a sexual nature. For this reason, the same principles of virtuous love and virtuous interactions with those of the opposite sex still apply, in any state of life and at any age.

Seminarians do well to think of themselves as akin to someone who is in a serious dating relationship—somewhere between courting and engagement. This means a seminarian should not be maintaining contact with, for example, old girlfriends in a way that would be inappropriate if he were in a serious relationship with someone else. Nor is it a good idea to call and text a young lady regularly if the seminarian has any indication that the young woman has romantic interest in him (but just hasn't said so explicitly for obvious reasons). Friendship is great and important; but we also have to be careful with other people's hearts—as well as our own.

To continue the analogy, a priest or religious does well to act as a married person would act. That is, for example, a priest's relationship with someone of the opposite sex shouldn't cross boundaries—physically or emotionally—that would be inappropriate if he were a married man, wedded to someone else.

While there can be a degree of spiritual and emotional intimacy in confession and spiritual direction that will be unique to religious life, as a great many religious have shared with us over the years, the key is keeping it in this "professional" setting. What is learned in spiritual direction must stay in spiritual direction and not become the basis for inappropriate intimacy, emotional or otherwise, outside of those confines.

In the end, whether one is single, married, or religious, it comes down to ensuring that one's friendships are built upon truth, grounded in real love. For *authentic love is always rooted in truth*—and that includes the objective truth of one's state in life and the vows one has taken.

Whether single, married, or religious, the danger arises when we elevate how we *feel* above the objective truth of the situation, leaving aside a sincere concern for the objective good of the other—which must always be rooted in truth (again, including the truth of their state in life).

What emerges in the human heart is all too often a selfish love that is engrossed in one's own experience of the other and the way the other makes us feel. This allows that experience to take precedence over all else. It allows feelings to run roughshod over truth and to triumph over authentic love. Despite how it might feel, this is really self-love in disguise.

In fact, "sinful love," in the words of John Paul II, is often saturated with emotion, which is what makes it so deceptive—because it can *feel* like the real thing:

> Sin is then born from the fact that man does not want to subordinate affection to the person and love, but on the contrary, he *subordinates the person and love to affection.* "Sinful love" is often very affective; it is saturated with affection, which supplants everything else in that love. Of course, its sinfulness does not lie in the fact of being saturated with

affection; it does not lie in affection itself, but in the fact that the will
places affection before the person, and this cancels all objective laws
and principles that must govern the union of persons, of a woman and
a man.[33]

It is easy for us to deceive ourselves, especially when things are kept "secret"
and in the dark. In marriage or religious life, we can even mask unhealthy
dynamics with overly "spiritual" conversation. Underneath, though, we
might be using the other person. He or she becomes not so much the
object of our sincere affection and goodwill but merely an "occasion" for us
to experience emotional gratification.[34] Self-deception is a powerful thing,
especially when it is masked by an apparently "spiritual" flavor.

Here is where it is so important for everyone in every state of life to develop
healthy male-female friendships. If our only experience of friendship with
the opposite sex is for ulterior motives, then we will not know how to
handle attractions to others when they arise. We will not know how to
engage and interact with the opposite sex in constructive and healthy
ways—that is, how to develop and foster *authentic* friendships with them.

There really is a virtue to living friendship well between the sexes, to
being able to see the other as intrinsically valuable *as a person.* This is the
enormous difference between authentic love and mere use.

For all these reasons, male-female friendships are holy and good—and
even essential for our growth. When lived well, they form us in important
ways, as we learn to interact with the opposite sex without sexualizing
them or using them for emotional gratification.

Indeed, this is a training in the school of authentic love, which is the
opposite of using.

Next, we will consider meaning and grit in dating. It is not hard to see the
link between friendship—especially with the opposite sex—and dating,
since both are about learning how to *love well.*

If authentic friendship is a training in the school of love, then it prepares us to navigate the dating scene in healthy and constructive ways, and even to handle things a little bit better if they don't go as planned.

PART IV

LIVING GIFT AND GRIT IN DATING

CHAPTER 9

WHO SHOULD I DATE AND HOW DO I GO ABOUT IT?

Sarah: We had been dating for months, and we had started seriously talking about marriage. It was such an exciting time. Things were "getting real," and both of us could sense it. We were out on a date night, and after dinner Swaff asked me to go on a walk. I remember us chatting about this and that, then suddenly Swaff stopped and turned to me, placing my hands in his. He looked me straight in the eye, and I could feel the intensity of his gaze. He said, "Sarah, I love you. I truly do. And I would do anything for you. But I am not perfect. I know that I will at times fail you. As much as I wish I could always take away your pain, I won't be able to. I can't be your everything, but I will always point you to the One who is your everything. I will always take you to the Lord. *I don't want us to run at each other—I want to run with you toward him,* toward heaven; and I want to take as many people as we can with us."

This was a pivotal moment in our relationship. I think Swaff could sense that there was still a part of my heart that needed this clarity and truth. Because, like so many others, I sometimes fell into the trap of thinking that finding a person—that special someone—would be the ultimate fulfillment and answer to my own version of "I'll be happy if and when."

Swaff tenderly reminded me of the great truth that our hearts find their fulfillment first in God. This conversation became a springboard for countless others, which led to some profound healing. As we have done for many others, we pass this gentle reminder on to you at the start of this chapter on dating—it is something that we still remind each other of to this day.

WHOLENESS (AND NEEDINESS) IN RELATIONSHIPS

We have a desire for infinite happiness. Whether we realize it or not, this is a desire for God, as he gently and gradually draws us back to himself. Many people run from relationship to relationship looking for something that is impossible to find—infinite happiness from a human relationship. This is a great way to destroy a relationship, because no relationship can bear the weight of our infinite desire. It was never meant to.

Dating is more like *multiplication* than *addition*. If two people are whole (i.e., they are seeking virtue and living on mission), when they come together, they can become one—united as a couple on mission together. But if they have not individually sought to live on mission, seeking virtue with intentionality and purpose (i.e., they have not become "whole" in this sense), then their coming together tends to result in something of a codependency, seeking happiness and fulfillment from each other, in a way only God can fulfill. Mathematically, $1 \times 1 = 1$ but $\frac{1}{2} \times \frac{1}{2} = \frac{1}{4}$. Here, two halves don't equal a whole, as they do in addition.

None of this was clear to us prior to our conversions. For most of our lives, it was so easy to think that finding the right relationship would be *the* thing that would usher us into definitive happiness and fulfillment.

The fact is when first things (i.e., God, virtue, living on mission) are put *first*, second things (e.g., relationships) are *not diminished* but *enhanced*. But when second things are put first, our lives fall into disarray and begin to implode.

Our conversation on that memorable date helped establish a mutual understanding that our relationship was rooted in a common mission, in our shared pursuit of virtue and holiness. Like a virtuous friendship, our relationship was *about something*—namely, running to our Lord together. This mission and purpose even provided accountability for us, whenever it seemed we were deviating from our goal.

With this groundwork, let's jump into the exciting but complicated world of dating.

"BUT I DON'T WANT TO LOSE OUR FRIENDSHIP"

Sometimes it seems obvious to everybody else as they look upon two people who seem to have a great deal of chemistry, and they ask, "So, why aren't they dating already?"

But the two people hesitate, often because they don't want to "lose their friendship."

Suppose you have a friend of the opposite sex, with whom you have a shared sense of mission, oriented around following Jesus wholeheartedly, and you connect well with this person. You may even have already begun to spend a decent amount of time with him or her. At this point, you might want to just enjoy what you have and don't want to lose it, so you never take the risk of seeing whether there might be something deeper in this relationship. In truth, you are already enjoying many of the benefits of a relationship, without the formal commitment.

On one occasion, we were at a restaurant and saw two people we knew. They looked like a couple out for dinner. As we chatted with them, they told us that they were on a "frate." As they saw our look of amusement, they explained that "frate" was short for "friend date." These "frates" have become quite common in recent years (whether or not people use this specific term), with some becoming even weekly occurrences that go on for months.

Here's the thing: A "friendship" like this is almost certainly not going to stay as it is forever, because life will "sift" these friendships. Inevitably, such a friendship will change when one of the two enters a serious relationship with someone else or eventually gets married to someone else. For this reason, we call this a *"friendship in motion."*

By the nature of things, this type of friendship is destined ultimately either to turn into a dating relationship or to change significantly, likely even fizzling out eventually. Why? Because the friendship has already *moved beyond mere friendship*, something that becomes clearer when we answer the following question:

Would the nature of the relationship between these two "friends" (i.e., their conversations, what they do together) be appropriate if either of them were in a serious dating relationship with someone else?

If the answer is "no," then they are not *just* friends.

This is Emotional Virtue 101.

The two people have entered the "gray zone" between friendship and dating, but they don't want to admit it. While this transition is inevitable to some extent, the key is to recognize it for what it is and not prolong it any longer than it needs to be.[35]

The worst thing we can do is insist that we are "just friends" but actually do the "pretend" dating thing (i.e., "frates")—living on and on in the gray zone between friendship and dating, sometimes for months (and even years).[36] When the friendship is prolonged in this way, it generally leads to confusion and heartache.

IS THE RISK WORTH IT?

Given that these friendships are not likely to remain as they are forever, there is *so much to gain and very little to lose* by taking the risk of seeing whether there might be something more than "friendship" between the two.

Is this scary?

Is it a risk?

Might it become awkward if the other person doesn't feel the same way?

Yes … yes … and yes!

But is it still worth the amazing possibility of what could be around the corner?

Definitely!

And again, what really is the alternative?

You could continue playing pretend for a while, calling yourselves "just friends"—and then, as things inevitably change later in life, find yourself haunted by the gigantic "what if" of what could have been. There is just so much to gain by taking a risk here. Life is simply too short not to. God will write straight with our crooked lines, but we need to put ourselves out there for him to do so.

The reality is that the same traits you have come to appreciate in your friend are likely similar to what you are looking for in a potential spouse. So, the question to ask is, *How much time are we wasting because we are afraid to take the risk?*

It is far better to take the risk and acknowledge our honest romantic interest. Don't worry about losing this "friendship" because, again, it is almost certainly going to change at some point anyway. After all, don't you secretly want to know whether this friendship could blossom into something really special?

In your heart of hearts, you might agree that this is a risk worth taking. But maybe you just need a little courage. Consider this your loving "nudge" from an older brother and sister in the Lord! Regardless of how it turns out, we are confident you will not regret giving it a try—but you may seriously regret it someday if you don't.

Here's the deal: If you date well by keeping your relationship pure, then it will not be that awkward to return to being friends if it doesn't work out. But if you date like the rest of the world, especially if the relationship becomes sexual, then things will definitely be awkward afterward. So it all depends on *how* we date.

DON'T SETTLE

Depending on our state in life, temptations will vary. As we grow older and have not found that special someone we are looking for, we might fall into the temptation of "settling" and lowering our standards. We might see our previously "high standards" as a hopeful and youthful ideal but one that seems all but impossible to attain. We might tell ourselves that we need to be more "realistic" about our prospects, that we need to make the best of a less-than-ideal situation.

While we sincerely understand the power of this temptation, especially as the years go by, the truth is *nothing good happens out of desperation.* In our down moments, we might think that happiness lies in the prospect of some future relationship, but the reality is *if we are not happy as a single man or woman, we will not be happy in a relationship.*

We have a good friend who came to this realization in a profound way. As she entered her thirties and was still single, she told us, "I would rather grow old as a single woman in love with Jesus than become desperate and end up in a disappointing marriage that drags me away from our Lord."

When it comes to discerning marriage and dating, the ultimate question is: *If something were to happen to you ten years into marriage and you were to pass away, would you trust this person with your kids, as the primary influence shaping their minds and hearts?*

It is easy to justify settling when we are thinking only about dating. We might imagine that we will be the ones to "balance things out," to bring the spiritual element to the relationship. But it is quite another thing when we think about raising children together.

By "not settling" here, we are referring to matters of faith and character. Your potential spouse should be someone you can build your life around, someone with meaning and grit, someone you can count on through tough times—someone you want to help form the minds and hearts of your children.

On a personal level, we couldn't imagine not being able to share the deepest part of who we are—our faith—with the person we love the most, the person with whom we are most intimate. We would be lying to you if we didn't tell you that it is the richest and most anchoring gift of our marriage. It is truly a blessing beyond measure to have a spouse who sees and cherishes the same truth, who cherishes our life in Christ and sees heaven as the goal of our family.

Whereas: *If you find yourself dating someone you cannot see yourself marrying, then you are not dating that person—you are dating heartache.*

CAN YOU BE TOO PICKY?

There is a bit of a paradox here. While we strongly advocate not settling in matters of faith and moral character, there is a way to err on the other side.

Earlier, we mentioned the need to be open to God surprising us regarding friendship, how great friendships sometimes can form between people who did not at first seem to be an obvious match. The same can be true when it comes to dating. We need to be open to God surprising us.

Maybe the guy doesn't have wavy blond hair or is the same height as you. Maybe her personality is different from the girl you thought you would end up with—she doesn't know what ESPN is or she doesn't like the same podcasts as you. Even if at first glance, the person God places in your life may not seem to be your "perfect type," it's still possible that something truly wonderful could develop, if only given the chance.

While attraction is essential, some forms of attraction may develop more slowly over time. Sometimes a deeper attraction can emerge only gradually as we get to know someone better.

These different levels of attraction can also influence each other. For example, when we become deeply attracted to a person's personality and character, he or she often becomes more physically appealing in our eyes.

Earlier, we made use of St. John Paul II's distinction between *sensuality* and *sentimentality*. Together, he refers to these as the "raw materials" for love because this is how love begins—with physical attraction, flirtation, chemistry, and romance. While sensuality and sentimentality are the raw materials for love, authentic and mature love must be brought out of them by an act of the will, firmly committed to the objective good of the other.[37]

As this kind of mature love forms, the will can utilize this "raw material" of physical and emotional attraction to bring something even more lasting out of it. But this mature love, rooted in the will, develops more slowly than attraction. Love—willing the other's good—must "catch up" and go beyond the mere enjoyment of the other's attractiveness, physically and emotionally.[38] By an act of the will, we learn to love authentically and not merely "feed" on the attractiveness of the other.

Intriguingly, John Paul II describes how, on the one hand, sometimes a surplus of "raw material" (i.e., intense physical attraction and instant emotional chemistry) can simply be *consumed*, resulting not in a great love forming but one which degenerates into mere use and eventually fizzles out (Hollywood comes to mind here). On the other hand, he describes how sometimes a truly great love can form on the basis of only "*modest raw material*" (some grandparents might come to mind here).[39] This is the difference between lust and authentic love—one *consumes*, the other *gives*.

The question for us then is this: *Are we open to the possibility of a great love surprising us, perhaps even being formed from what at first struck us as only "modest raw material"?* For our secular culture, love can only be built upon an explosive concentration of "raw materials"—especially sexual attraction. But if we are open to God surprising us, we do well to be open to the possibility that the Lord may bring about a great love in ways we did not initially expect.

While it is essential for us to be attracted to our spouse, we also need to consider the ways in which our culture may have skewed our perception of love and beauty and affected what we find attractive.

There is no doubt that pornography has distorted many men's perception of beauty in women. We should point out the crazy relativity here: pin-up models of the 1950s would be considered overweight today! This puts insane pressure on women. And when most models are a size 0 (or close to it), this sets men up for disappointment since no woman actually looks like the flawless, photoshopped models they are scrolling through on their screens. If we want to think objectively about the natural order, curves are part of the feminine genius—as they facilitate the miracle of family and childbirth.

A friend of ours who works extensively with university students has suggested that social media seems to have also influenced women's romantic expectations. After a steady diet of emotionally charged beautiful weddings, proposals, vacations, and day-to-day expressions of romance and beauty, it is not hard to see why women's expectations would rise, as each woman wants to be made to feel as special as the portrayals she sees on the screen. And she likely also wants to be able to post about these experiences as well and receive admiration and validation that way. Of course, the rise of pornography among women has also had an impact, and social media has no doubt had its influence upon the emotional expectations of men as well.

Whether we are considering sensuality (i.e., physical attraction) or sentimentality (i.e., emotional attraction), our secular culture has shaped and tweaked what each sex perceives as beautiful, charming, and attractive—and not always for the better!

This gives us all the more reason to allow the Lord to purify our minds and hearts, to purify what we perceive as beautiful and attractive. With this purification comes an openness to the possibility of God surprising us in ways we did not at first expect.

"I'VE NEVER BEEN ASKED OUT. WHAT IS WRONG WITH ME?"

Over the years, our hearts have broken over the number of times we have heard from wonderful Catholic women *who say they have never been asked on a single date throughout their entire collegiate years.*

Much of the reason seems to stem from some of the issues already discussed in this chapter. Many men, for example, are afraid of "losing their friendship," and so they never take the next step toward dating, or they are a bit too picky for the wrong reasons.

Or, to go back to the previous chapter, perhaps we need more groups of male friends and female friends joining together with a clear sense of mission (more *Środowisko*), which tends to be a natural place for strong relationships to emerge and take shape.

But there seems to be another reason as well. We hear from many good Catholic men that they find themselves intimidated by virtuous, confident Catholic women.

Many of these men confide in us that they do not feel worthy to date such women, whom they sincerely respect and admire. They often feel like they need to hit moral perfection before they can even begin to broach the possibility of dating some of these amazing women.

While some things need to be attended to individually first before we are ready to date, a distinction needs to be made here. There is a vast difference between someone who has grown accustomed to serious, habitual sin (e.g., pornography, masturbation, binge drinking, etc.) and has therefore become apathetic and indifferent to making real progress in the spiritual life, and the person who is sincerely striving for holiness but has occasional falls that bring him to his knees—which then become catalysts for renewed zeal, conversion, and repentance.

In other words, there is a big difference between *lukewarmness* and someone who is sincerely *striving for virtue and holiness*.

If we are not striving for holiness—striving to "run so as to win" (1 Corinthians 9:24, NABRE)—then we are not ready to date. We cannot build a holy and virtuous relationship until we are serious about holiness and virtue ourselves.

But striving is not the same as becoming a saint first.

Here are a few questions we can ask to help clarify the difference (either in ourselves or in the person we are considering dating):

- *Does this person sincerely hate the sin with which he or she is struggling, and do they desire to avoid it at all costs? Is he or she serious about taking the practical steps to avoid the situations that trigger their falling into that particular sin?*

- *Is he or she investing in virtuous friendships—with sincere availability, vulnerability, and accountability?*

- *Does he or she desire to live with Jesus at the center of every aspect of his or her life? This includes their use of media, the music they listen to, and the conversations they have, as well as their friendships and relationships. Do they desire Jesus to truly be Lord of their entire mind and heart?*

- *Is there a commitment to regular prayer and ongoing Christian formation of their mind and heart?*

We are not talking about perfection, but about someone who sincerely *wants* it with all their heart.

If the answer to the above questions is "yes," then the man who might be struggling with confidence needs to put aside his false humility and pursue the wonderful, virtuous Catholic woman in his life. He needs to reject the lie that he is not worthy to approach her.

Gentlemen, there is great joy and liberation ahead if you take the risk and believe in yourselves—believe in the power of Christ's life flowing through you. *Take the risk and ask her out.* You have far less to lose than you can imagine and far more to gain than you could ever fathom.

Andrew: After my conversion, what I realized was that the whole purpose of dating is to discern marriage. In that context, my new friends and I really changed how we thought about the prospects of rejection. While still scary, we realized that if she says no, then that is *clarity*—which is *literally the goal.* This doesn't make it easy, but it helps put it into perspective.

CAN THE LADY MAKE THE ASK?

In a way, yes.

Many Catholics and Christians have long discussed the man's role as *pursuer* and the woman's complementary desire to be *pursued.* There is something fundamentally right about this, something that flows from our natures as men and women.

Too often, though, this leads to the ladies sitting on the sidelines—as wallflowers, as it were, quietly waiting for some future man to spot them from a distance and race toward them with exuberant confidence—maybe even on a white horse!

So, what's the problem here?

Catholic men struggling with confidence are not going to approach this amazing Catholic woman who at first glance seems to have zero interest in him. The first recommendation for the ladies, then, is to *feel free to drop a hint.*

Sarah: Women have always "dropped the handkerchief," as it were, by finding subtle ways to express interest in a particular man. I have been thinking about what the modern-day equivalent may be. Perhaps single ladies should carry two cell phones, the one they actually use and an old one they "accidentally drop" near a particular young man. When he sees her drop her phone, he will rush to pick it up for her, and suddenly, the two might have a conversation. Who knows, maybe sparks will fly?

Of course, there is an art to dropping hints and certainly not one way to do it. But there is a need for men and women to find subtle ways to express interest in the other. This is not the same as walking up to the other person and blurting out: "Will you date me?" But dropping hints is the way human relationships have always begun, and we're naive to think they will readily happen otherwise.

DTR — "DEFINE THE RELATIONSHIP"

In our experience, there are ultimately two *DTR ("define the relationship")* moments. The first is an initial showing of interest. This can be as simple as saying to someone: "I really appreciate our friendship, and I would like to get to know you better. Maybe we can get coffee and chat more sometime?" Ladies, if a guy says that to you, he is most likely not looking to just be your friend.

Making a point to get a drink or coffee with someone one-on-one (even more so if a meal is involved) is almost certainly not an act of mere friendship. One can definitely think of exceptions here. But if someone goes out of their way to initiate this, you are best to take it as an indication of some romantic interest. For all intents and purposes, this is a *date*.

The second DTR comes when a commitment is made; this resolves the "what are we?" question. Moving from the transition of friendship to getting to know the other person better in order to see whether there might be a romantic future is what the "gray area" is all about. This "in-between" time is inevitable to some extent; but the key, as we have said before, is not prolonging it any longer than it needs to be.[40]

If we are intentional about getting to know someone better—moving from friendship toward the prospects of dating—this shouldn't take more than a few weeks or maybe a month or so. At that point, we either need to go through with it and start dating, or we need to back off. What we shouldn't do is continue with our *coffee get-to-know-you sessions* for months (and even years), pretending to be "just friends" and scheduling regular "frates" ("friend dates")—ultimately because we are afraid to take the risk and actually define the relationship.

For our part, *it doesn't matter who expresses the initial showing of interest* (the first DTR)—the woman or the man. Frankly, it is better to get the ball rolling and see what is there with sincerity and clarity. Clarity is far more important than whatever supposed "ideal" we may have in our minds as to how this process is supposed to look.

Call us old-fashioned, but we think the man should initiate the second DTR. He should take the lead—and the risk—of saying to the woman in effect: "I want to commit to you, and I would like to know if you feel the same way."

On the one hand, the danger in saying that it doesn't matter who makes the ask is that this can be a crutch for guys and make them lazy. On the other hand, the danger of being overly idealistic in insisting that the man should be the initiator at every stage (with no "dropping of the handkerchief" or hints of any kind) is that nobody ends up asking anybody out, and the dating process never gets off the ground.

So, for the initial showing of interest, the first DTR, either the guy or girl can initiate. Regarding the second DTR, the stage of commitment, the man needs to put himself out there, facing head-on the fear of rejection or the prospect of something new and beautiful emerging.

Deep down, a man truly wants this classic "no guts, no glory" moment, despite his trepidation leading up to it. Men want a battle to fight; they want something worthwhile to go after. Deep down, they want something—and someone—worth *risking* for. A man taking a risk by asking a lady he is interested in if she feels the same way certainly fits this bill.

If the first DTR has already taken place, then you certainly have something to go on. Most likely, you have some idea where she stands.

So, make it official. Give her the chance to see you take the risk for her sake. You will not regret it in the end.

For the record, when a man does this and gets rejected, his sense of honor does not decrease but actually *increases*—because of his display of courage in his willingness to put himself out there. In fact, if he takes this rejection well, it is especially worthy of praise, as it represents a very mature and high degree of character on his part—bravery for putting himself out there and a gentleman's humility in graciously accepting no for an answer. In fact, it is a tremendous display of strength when a man can receive rejection and not allow it to totally wreck his confidence (or cause him to become vindictive and petty toward the woman). This is a man who will be able to receive constructive criticism well—say, from a boss or superior, a trait that is unfortunately becoming less and less common. Even in rejection, the man is engaging in a heroic battle and growing in profound ways, demonstrating a humble and gracious confidence.

Ladies, please understand how gut-wrenching this can be for a man. This is where your dropping "hints" can dramatically bolster his confidence— they are a subtle way of inviting the ask. Gentlemen, please understand what this means for a woman. To be pursued and chosen is a fundamental desire of every human being, but this is especially so for women.

If you are interested in her, give her this honor—you will not regret it, and it will mean the world to her (as long as you are sincere).

Here is an example that reinforces our point. A group of Benedictine College students, along with some faculty members and their spouses, put on a traditional English dance on campus. There was a professional instructor and music—it felt like we had stepped into a Jane Austen novel!

The tickets to the event were evenly distributed among men and women, and the instructor made it clear that for each new dance, the gentleman had to ask a lady—and with each new song, everyone had to switch partners.

Afterward, many of the women said that *their favorite part was simply being asked.*

Gentleman, the ladies obviously want to be *chosen*, *asked*, and *cherished*. You won't regret giving them this honor.

SINCERITY AND CLARITY

When it comes to dating, we like to tell people to repeat the words *"sincerity"* and *"clarity."* Whether our dating experience is enriching and fulfilling, or whether it becomes a "game" with no one really knowing what's going on, usually resulting in someone getting hurt—sincerity and clarity can make all the difference.

For this reason, it is best to pursue only one person at a time. After an answer emerges between the two of you—the relationship is either getting more serious or you have decided to back off—then you can consider the possibility of pursuing someone else in this way. Whereas, when you are taking multiple people on coffee dates or even to dinner, this can result in confusion and even heartache, as people don't know exactly where you stand and what your intentions are. *Clarity* is lacking, and your *sincerity* can be open to question.

WHAT IF I HAVE DROPPED EVERY HINT IN THE BOOK?

Sometimes ladies will ask us: "What if I have dropped every hint in the book and the guy has not responded?" What should a woman do if a guy is simply not responding at all?

Andrew: In general, guys can be dense—but not as dense as you might think. If a lady has dropped multiple hints on several occasions, at some point the woman needs to take this as a "hint" in return that the guy is just not interested.

While there might be exceptions, this is true often enough that we would counsel the woman not to tie her heart in knots over what she would like to see develop, but rather accept the fact that he doesn't seem to feel the same way and begin to move on.

You never know who or what you might be missing out on if you keep trying to force something that simply isn't there. *You don't want to be in love with someone who only wants to be your friend.*

WHAT IS THE SECRET SAUCE?

At the end of the day, three factors need to come together for a relationship to work—*God, chemistry,* and *timing.*[41]

If we are not putting God at the center of our lives, pursuing virtue, and living on mission, then we are not ready to date. The same is true of the significant other we would really like to date. *If God is not at the center of their lives, then he or she is not ready to be the person you are truly looking for.*

Sometimes two people might be amazing individuals, who both have the Lord as the center of their lives and are living on mission. On paper, the relationship looks perfect. However, when they are together, something seems off. Simply put, they don't have the right *chemistry* for the makings of a strong relationship. Chemistry is a bit hard to define—but you know it when you see it (and you also know when it's lacking). If something is off, it's best not to try and "force" it. Figuring this part out is exactly why you date. Concluding that the chemistry between the two of you is not right is *not* a failure, nor is it a knock against either person—it's about discerning whether the two of you are compatible. Remember, every relationship ends either in marriage or with a breakup. If you have discerned well, either option is ultimately a good thing (even if it doesn't feel like it in the moment).

And sometimes two lives just can't be coordinated very well at the moment. Maybe one is overseas, in the midst of graduate school, or coming out of a bad relationship. In other words, the *timing* may just be off.

When *God*, *chemistry*, and *timing* come together, the recipe is there for a great relationship to form, maybe even the beginnings of what will become a lifelong marriage.

THE "ELEPHANT" IN THE ROOM: ONLINE DATING

As you have been reading up to this point, you may have been wondering, "But what about online dating?"

Let's face it—people often meet each other differently today than they used to. Friends, professionals, and even moms' groups frequently find each other online, even if they live in the same area.

If you desire marriage, it is worth pursuing the possibility of meeting someone online, especially through Catholic dating sites. Of course, you will want to use appropriate filters to make sure you have an accurate impression of who a person is and how serious he or she is about a life of faith and virtue.

Making an online profile is a clear way of giving a "hint"—it signals that you have an interest in dating and would like to be pursued. It is a great way to meet someone who may already live in your city but whom you may not meet otherwise. Or this special someone may live in a whole different part of the country, and you would almost certainly never cross paths otherwise.

Still, online dating has its challenges. For example, it is much more difficult to establish a friendship before dating. In addition, you do not have the security of knowing their reputation and friends ahead of time. You are really forced to get to know them solely through the dating process.

For this reason, as things progress, it will be important to get to know their family and friends in order to see what their life is like apart from you. After all, someone might impress you when you are together, and then prove to be a different person altogether when you're not around.

In the end, it will be important to spend time together, living in the same city, to fully gauge who this person is and discover the true depth of your relationship. There are ultimately some aspects of a relationship that cannot be adequately discerned from afar.

For these reasons, we are all for *online meeting* but *in-person dating*, especially as the relationship becomes more serious. We have seen many examples of incredible marriages come from online dating—which is wonderful and amazing.

But for some, online dating takes a certain amount of humility. We have met people who shudder at the thought of resorting to meeting someone online. They have said things like: "I don't want our story as a couple to start with, 'We met online' or, 'We met on social media.'" It seems they have the sense that meeting online somehow implies they were deficient in some way—as if they were desperate and unable to make it happen the "normal way."

Frankly, life is too short for such concerns. The world has changed, and so has the dating scene. Many people meet in the traditional way. For others, online dating may be the best and most efficient way for something to work out.

Wouldn't it be better to find the spouse you're looking for online than end up "settling" for someone who doesn't want to live on mission with you and isn't really what you were hoping for?

What matters more—the "story" we think we should have about how we met, *or the faith and character of our spouse*? We should not let our pride or vanity get in the way; we want to be truly open to God surprising us.

We will never regret being open to the Lord's "surprises," but we may well regret closing ourselves off from what he may have planned for us.

CHAPTER 10

BREAKUPS CAN BE BRUTAL—HOW CAN I MOVE ON WHEN I KEEP LOOKING BACK?

Over the past few years, we have looked at each other many times and said, "We have to write something on breakups." It is the number one thing we both get questions about and the number one thing we help people through. It is an honor to accompany men and women through some of the toughest times of their lives, because breakups can be absolutely brutal.

Though this chapter is about breakups, this entire book is actually our answer to how to heal from a breakup. We don't pretend to have all the answers, and we don't take this subject lightly. But we want you to know that you don't walk this road alone.

When you have spent a great deal of time with someone—and even started planning your life around them—it is tremendously painful to have this stable and predictable part of your life ripped away.

When we are hurt, we are tempted to resolve never to let ourselves be vulnerable again. We are tempted to never trust again, to never love again.

As the dust settles and enough time has gone by, hopefully we are able to see the truth that the *risk of love* is always worth it—and that life is not about sitting on the sidelines and playing "defense." Living life to its fullest means taking reasonable risks, and one of those risks is love. We cannot let our hurt keep us from playing the game of life with everything we have, in search of everything life has to offer.

But how do we practically take the next step—how do we start anew when it hurts so badly?

While this is never easy, there are things we can do (and not do) that will make a big difference.

WHAT ABOUT AFTER WE BREAK UP— CAN WE STILL BE FRIENDS?

We cannot begin to tell you how many times we have been asked this question over the past decade! Indeed, navigating this part well can significantly impact your ability to begin healing and moving forward.

The answer to this question depends a great deal on how the dating process went and how long you were together. The more sexual it turned, the more difficult it will be for a genuine friendship to continue. And even if the dating process went well, there will still need to be a good bit of time before a friendship can continue.

One can certainly have goodwill toward an ex—wishing him or her well and being cordial to one another. This is different, though, from having an ongoing friendship, with regular communication and involvement in each other's lives.

While it can be tough, it is generally not a good idea to maintain regular communication right after a breakup, acting almost as if the breakup never really occurred. For one thing, regular interaction and hanging out can easily turn sexual (especially if there has been a sexual past between the two). This doesn't create clarity but exacerbates confusion—making it harder to move on and start anew.

Even though difficult, the best thing to do after a breakup is to have a period of no contact. There needs to be closure for both of you that the relationship is over. When this doesn't happen, either one or both people never really begin the process of healing and moving forward.

At this point, it is easy for one or both people to simply use each other, either emotionally or physically (or both). This situation can linger, sometimes for a long time, because we do not want to lose the attention and emotional gratification we were used to receiving. When we have come to count on things such as having someone check in on us, message us, or plan our days or weekends around them, it is tempting to continue seeking these comforts from an ex. But this is using him or her emotionally, and it inevitably leads to greater heartache in the end. We reach out to an ex because we are afraid to be alone. But this will not help us heal; it will only prolong our pain and keep us from healing and moving on to the next chapter in our life.

Even after a significant period has gone by, we must still be careful about the nature of the communication that takes place between us and our ex. As a rule, we advise that communication never get more intimate than would be appropriate if either one of you were in a serious relationship with someone else. While this might sound drastic, we can easily deceive ourselves by pretending that our motives are pure and that we are "just friends." In reality, our hearts might be bursting at the seams, yearning for intimacy with our ex (emotional or otherwise).

THE KEYS TO MOVING ON

While nothing will ever undo the initial pain of a breakup, here are a few things to keep in mind as we try to move forward.

First, we need to recognize that there are *seasons in life*. Just as fall and winter eventually give way to spring and summer, the same is true in life. The great lie we're tempted to believe here is that our down times will last *forever* (which only compounds our suffering). But this is not true. Remembering the seasonal nature of life goes a long way toward being able to get through hard times. We know that our "winter" will eventually turn to "spring" and then "summer"; knowing that a hard time will not last forever already provides a spark of confidence. Recognizing the ebb and flow of life enables us to use the high times to strengthen ourselves in preparation for future low points that will inevitably come our way.[42]

Second, it is worth going back to the basics and remembering that *no human being can ever fulfill us or make us happy.* As we mentioned, *if we can't find happiness as a single, we'll never find it in a relationship.* The best relationships come about when two people are individually whole and both recognize that they have been made for the infinite, not ultimately for any finite human being. This enables us to avoid a codependent or exaggerated neediness of the other.

In the context of a breakup, as great as our heartache is, we know that this relationship was never the ultimate source of our happiness. It never could be.

But at the time of our breakup, we probably won't *feel* this truth, and we might not for a long time. By keeping it in mind, we can allow it to begin penetrating our hearts. Reflecting upon this truth is necessary before, during, and after a relationship—but especially after a breakup.

Third, we need to ask ourselves: *Who (or what) are we missing out on while our hearts are so firmly stuck in the past?*

We might miss out on the person in love with us—if we insist on clinging to the person who wants to be no more than our friend. Often, it takes one door to close for a new one to open.

Andrew: When I walked away from my old relationship, I had no idea that I would meet the woman who would become my wife almost a year later. But if I had not followed the Lord's promptings when I did, I wouldn't have been ready or open to the blessing of meeting Sarah. We never know the full story unfolding before our eyes. Even though it might hurt and be scary, we do not know what is around the corner. And we will never find out if our hearts are stuck in the past, trying to prop up something that is actually dying.

As harsh as it may sound, *a breakup brings clarity*. Even though painful, we should embrace this clarity as "gift" as much as we can. *Sarah:* When my boyfriend cheated on me, as much as this hurt, it definitely brought me deep clarity.

The truth is gaining clarity, even through a breakup, is an answer to the fundamental purpose of dating. Even if it's not the answer we were hoping for, this clarity is a gift—and the sooner it comes, the better.

So, in summary, to pick up the pieces and move forward after a breakup, we need to recognize that:

- *There are seasons in life.*
- *A relationship with a human being can never be the most important thing in our life or the ultimate source of our happiness.*
- *We need to reflect on who or what we are missing out on by keeping our hearts stuck in the past. The clarity of a breakup is a net positive: if this door was meant to close, the sooner it closes the better, so we can start healing and welcome the new doors the Lord will open for us.*

In the end, there is no substitute for time. Immediately after a breakup, we might feel like we cannot even breathe. But after a week, it might be a little better, and yet still very raw and painful. It is helpful to think in terms of *seven days, seven weeks, seven months*. Focus on small goals—small increments of healing—which will add up over time. Each of the above increments will give way to new thresholds of healing and recovery.

Real healing takes time, which is why we need to be patient with ourselves and with God's ongoing work in our hearts.

LEARNING FROM THE PAST

As time goes by, we should try to learn from the relationship that has just ended. What went well? What didn't go so well? What pitfalls did we fall into?

Eventually, we may be able to see more clearly that something was a little bit off. We might be able to recall the "red flags" that we may have ignored or pushed aside, which we can now see more clearly. Learning from this experience will enable us to recognize these warning signs earlier on in future relationships.

This experience can help us understand what we want and need in a future spouse. While the objective criteria—faith, virtue, character—are of first importance, more goes into marriage than simply an objective checklist (e.g., "chemistry"). We should make the most of this experience by allowing it to sharpen our discernment for the future.

For all these reasons, we should recognize that it may have been God's will for us to date a certain person, even if the relationship didn't work out. Maybe there was something each person was called to learn that only came to light through this dating process.

SEASONS OF SINGLENESS

Though it may not feel like it, the season of singleness has its own unique charism and dynamism. This period can be a distinct time of growth—in prayer, friendship, and divinely inspired self-discovery.

Radical "self-discovery" in the secular sense can be self-centered and narcissistic; but self-discovery in the context of faith—and a deep sense that our lives are not ultimately about us—can be a profound and godly endeavor.

Here is the thing: It is difficult to change and grow in the midst of people who have deeply ingrained notions and expectations of who you are. This can be true of old friends, as well as family members. *And this is especially true when it comes to a significant other.* For this reason, the time of singlehood can be a unique opportunity for growth and maturation— for deepening the person you are and moving toward the person you are called to be.

The time of singlehood can be a time of deep self-enrichment, not for selfish motives but to give ourselves away more fully in love, so that we can make the most complete gift of ourselves someday. As our vocations become crystallized, for example, in marriage or religious life, the nature of our self-gift comes into sharper focus; living our time of singlehood well prepares us to bring more to the table when that time comes.

The season of singlehood is essential for making our self-gift all that it can be. Through our growth in virtue, prayer, friendship, study, and even the development of interests and hobbies, our self-offering becomes enriched. We are becoming "bigger on the inside," as we prepare to give ourselves away more fully in love.

KEEPING "GIFT" AT THE CENTER

The deep truth at the most fundamental level of reality is that *all is gift*, starting with creation itself.

Everyone, whether married, religious, or single, needs to hear this. Much resentment builds precisely because we assume, even subconsciously, that *we are owed something*—that we are *entitled* to something. The more this sentiment builds, the more *wronged* we feel when we do not have what we want—what we feel we deserve.

No matter how devoted we are to the Lord, this sentiment can find a foothold within us and can increase steadily over time. It is easy to think, "I have been a good Catholic. I have done all the right things, and I have seen all my friends get happily married. *When will it be my turn?*"

This attitude can affect us at any stage in life. But we are especially prone to it when we are single.

For the sake of your walk with the Lord, try as hard as you can to grow in your awareness that *all is gift*—from creation and salvation, to the ordinary day-to-day. The deeper our sense of this truth, the more you will be open to God surprising you—and the more peace and joy you will experience.

When we look back, we will want to see this period of singleness as a time of growth, honing our sense of meaning and grit. Seeing our entire lives as gift dramatically facilitates our ability to grow, whereas the bitterness that follows from feeling like life (and God) has wronged us tends to hinder our growth. We become more focused on *what we don't have*, instead of being attentive to all that God is doing in our lives in the present.

God is doing a great work in you—a great work in all of us. But it might look different from what we expected.

THE EXAMPLE OF JAN TYRANOWSKI

This is a man who stole our hearts. Jan Tyranowski was born in Poland in 1901 and became a key mentor to Karol Wojtyła (the future St. John Paul II) during the Nazi occupation of World War II.

In 1935, Tyranowski heard a homily from a Salesian priest with a line that pierced his heart: "It's not hard to be a saint." Though he was a practicing Catholic, at this moment he went "all in," diving deeply into prayer and the spiritual life, especially the writings of St. John of the Cross and St. Teresa of Avila.

Tyranowski's parish in Krakow, St. Stanislaus Kostka, had a significant youth outreach. This was the parish Karol Wojtyła and his father attended when they moved to Krakow for his university studies. In May of 1941, when Wojtyła was twenty-one, the Nazis rounded up the priests from St. Stanislaus parish and sent them to concentration camps. At this point, the parish's youth outreach went underground and fell to lay leaders, including Jan Tyranowski.

Tyranowski developed what was known as the "Living Rosary," consisting of groups of fifteen young men of high school and college age. In addition to praying the Rosary with them, Tyranowski instructed them in prayer and helped form them in the virtues, based on the spirituality of St. John of the Cross. He became a mentor to these young men, and they formed deep friendships under his tutelage. They later remembered him as someone who taught the Faith not merely as an idea but as a living reality—as a personal encounter with God—which gave these young men light during such a dark and horrific time.

By 1943, there were sixty young men in these Living Rosary groups, ten of whom eventually became priests—including Karol Wojtyła.[43]

Tyranowski died shortly after World War II in 1947. He died as a single man, and he quite literally *changed the world*. Consider that without Tyranowski's mentorship, Karol Wojtyła may have never entered seminary; he easily could have pursued a career in theater and as a literary scholar instead (as he had previously intended). Then *there would never have been a Pope John Paul II*. The importance of Tyranowski's influence simply cannot be overstated.

In 1948, Wojtyła defended his doctoral dissertation on St. John of the Cross, just one of the many ways Tyranowski had an enduring influence upon the future pope.

Later in life, whenever St. John Paul II thought about the universal call to holiness and the lay apostolate (important emphases of Vatican II), his shining example was always Tyranowski.[44]

Tyranowski could have been bitter and jaded as a single young adult, disappointed in the way his life had turned out—and then he would never have made the impact he did. His radical yes to God in 1935, when he had no idea what lay around the corner (i.e., the Nazi occupation), enabled him to make his world-altering contribution to the Church. Most of us never really know how important our roles are in God's plan, but saying yes to his will again and again in the little things in the present moment is what makes it possible for us to carry out heroic tasks later. This certainly was the case with Jan Tyranowski.

We will never forget the times we have prayed at Tyranowski's tomb, located in the church of St. Stanislaus Kostka. We will especially never forget bringing our Florence students—our *Środowisko*—there to pray. The students already knew Tyranowski's story from class. They really took to him, seeing in him a shining example of living the single life well—with peace, joy, and strength. Praying before his remains brought so many of our students (and us!) to tears.

Sarah: I was so moved that, when we got back on the bus, I picked up the microphone and said, "I know you all want to do big things for God and that's beautiful—but when will you let him do big things for you? Let go of control and let God surprise you. You never know what he is preparing you for!"

God's "surprise" for Tyranowski was not simply a spouse he would soon meet, with whom he would live happily ever after. That *might* be his surprise for some of us, but it might not be. Whatever the Lord has planned, we know it will be profoundly meaningful. And our peace and joy will be greatest when we fully embrace the life God calls us to live in the present, not the one we think we *should* be living.

Life is a mystery, guided by the twists and turns of God's providence. We see partially, but not fully (see 1 Corinthians 13:12). For this reason, we need to be as flexible as we can in order to be open to whatever calling the Lord has for us.

Our calling—our vocation—is a *gift to be received, not a problem to be solved.* Receiving this gift requires us to unclench our hands, so that we are not rigidly grasping on to what we think his plan is *supposed* to be. We need to be open and ready to be surprised by the Lord, willing to accept whatever gifts he brings. Without this openness, we lose our peace and joy. We are then tempted to *grasp*, and anxiety sets in.

This does not make it easy or less painful to face the reality of a breakup or to find ourselves single. But the best way to soften this sting is to place our dreams and hopes in the wider framework of a God who loves us and made us for more than anything we could dream up ourselves.

We truly have been made for so much more than we realize.

Sometimes our dreams and plans need to be crucified, so that the Lord can resurrect the blessings *he* has planned for us. When we do—and let go of our desire for control—we will find the resurrected glory of something new and unexpected around the corner.

CHAPTER 11

CHASTITY IS CRUCIAL—
BUT WHY IS IT SO
DANG DIFFICULT?

Most of us have heard a chastity talk of some kind at some point, but it is another experience altogether to be the one giving it!

Sarah: I am blessed to get to travel and share my heart with people of all different ages. On more than one occasion, I have walked into a high school, checked into the office, and turned the corner, only to see a huge poster with my face on it—with an announcement listed below my picture: "Sarah Swafford – 2pm – Gym – Chastity Speaker." In my head, I'm thinking, "Oh, come on! Please, can you try to make me just a little bit cooler!?"

Chastity is not the easiest topic to talk about (at any age), and it is not just for junior high and high school students. Chastity is essential to living a life of meaning and grit. It affects all of us, in every walk of life—and for our whole life.

Actually, temptations against chastity can get stronger as one gets older, especially as one moves into their late twenties and thirties. We have seen many good people enter the professional world, and having been removed from their support system, they easily succumb to sexual temptation in relationships. They say things like, "Well, we're adults and we're in love," or, "We'll probably get married anyway."

Often, this is connected to the temptation to "settle" in a relationship. It is easy to conclude that "this is just how things are," feeling as though if you didn't compromise here, you'll never find the love you're looking for.

Sometimes we hear from Catholics who have given their lives to the Church—youth ministers, missionaries, theology teachers, directors of religious education—who also struggle in living chaste lives. Their sense of living a double life only compounds their sense of shame.

As the Church knows all too well, no person or institution is immune from sin. Sexual desire is a powerful, God-given force. It is like a glorious blaze meant to burn brightly in the fireplace, radiantly warming the whole house. But if you take away the fireplace—that is, if you remove sex from its proper context in marriage—the fire quickly burns down the entire house, and people end up getting hurt.

SEX, LOVE, AND DISCERNMENT

Let's say you are dating, and you think this person is the kind of person you would like to end up with. So now you are trying to navigate the next steps in the relationship.

At this point, you need to be especially vigilant regarding chastity, more than you might realize. While it is natural for physical affection to progress as the relationship continues, we need to be very careful—*because the body will follow the heart*. At this point, we will have plenty of excuses we can tell ourselves (e.g., "but we love each other," "everyone else seems to be OK with this, even good Catholics," etc.).

Sex is a binding and blinding force. It unites a couple and gives them "love goggles," as we used to say. This is part of its God-given beauty and power. Precisely because of its power, sex can mask real issues and often make couples *feel* like they are closer than they really are. Many of us have probably seen at one time or another how sex can prop up a relationship, making it last much longer than it likely would have otherwise.

Have you ever known a couple who seemed to fight endlessly, causing everyone to wonder how and why they were still together? Yet the relationship continued month after month, even year after year. It's common for sexual activity to be at the root of helping such a relationship continue longer than it otherwise would have.

The truth is this: Sex before marriage does not bring clarity but clouds our ability to see the truth of the relationship. As a binding force, sex can easily lead us to overlook problems that may be surfacing and can make us think things are better off than they really are—it can make us *feel* like the relationship is deeper and stronger than it really is.

CHASTITY AND LOVE

Ultimately, chastity is not simply a "no"; it is not mere abstinence. *Chastity is a great "yes."* The "no" it requires stems from a prior and more fundamental "yes," just as a married couple's "yes" to one another is the reason why they say "no" to sex with anybody else.

So, what is the "yes" of chastity for the non-married person?

It is the "yes" of true love—the "yes" to respecting the dignity of the other person and being firmly committed to *not using them*. It is about allowing a deeper love to develop—one that is focused first and foremost on the good of the other, loving the other for their own sake and not merely for what they can do for us.

After all, anyone can have sex with someone. That is not difficult to do.

But if someone is willing to deny themself and say no to sex for the sake of your purity—*because they love you* and don't want to use you—*what could this person not do for you?*

As countercultural as it is, doesn't this scream "total self-giving love" in a manner far more compelling than merely sleeping with you? The battle for real chastity is nothing short of heroic. Deep down most people know this is true, even if they would rather not live it out themselves.

True love is always *gift* love; it is always willing the good of the other person. It is never an attempt to *take* something from them.

Sex before marriage is always using because it is a *taking* love, where we seek the other as a good that "fills us up," not for their own sake. It is not a *giving* love, because it places our own desire for sexual and emotional intimacy ahead of the objective good of the other person. Even if it might *feel* like the real thing, it is really just self-love in disguise.

Sometimes two people can use each other in this way. When this happens, both are placing their experience—how they feel and their own desires—above the objective good of the other person. It is worthwhile returning to the following passage from St. John Paul II, about how sinful love typically places one's emotional (and physical) experience *above* the person:

> Sin is then born from the fact that man does not want to subordinate affection to the person and love, but on the contrary, he *subordinates the person and love to affection.* "Sinful love" is often very affective [i.e., emotional]; it is saturated with affection, which supplants everything else in that love. Of course, its sinfulness does not lie in the fact of being saturated with affection; it does not lie in affection itself, but in the fact that the will *places affection before the person,* and this cancels all objective laws and principles that must govern the union of persons, of a woman and a man.[45]

It takes incredible strength—and becomes a heroic witness—when someone puts your good above what they want in the moment. This is precisely how chastity becomes the *friend of love,* enabling and empowering a deeper love.

Chastity is the virtue that frees us to love the other for who they are and not merely for what they can do for us.[46]

Chastity only becomes a foe of love when we reduce love to nothing more than an emotional and physical experience. If that is all love is, then of course chastity gets in the way. But such a love never transcends *using* because it never rises above our seeking out the other for anything more than the fulfillment of our own desires, physical or emotional. If love is just a feeling—just an emotional and physical experience—then that *experience* is really what we are seeking, not the other person for their own sake.

But if love is an *act of the will*—willing the good of the other in total self-giving love—then chastity is the necessary virtue that liberates our love from using; it liberates us from the overpowering dominance of our own egotistical desire.[47] Chastity, then, becomes the virtue that makes authentic love possible—*it frees us to truly love.*

BUT HOW FAR IS "TOO FAR"?

Sarah: I remember walking by the door of the classroom when Swaff was teaching in Italy, and I could hear him taking questions about oral sex. I am confident that these students never asked questions like that before in a classroom! As we said, Florence was a unique experience. Many of these students never had someone with whom they felt comfortable asking such uncomfortable questions. In Florence, though, they felt free. And in this context, they also were open to being challenged—because they knew it came from us out of a place of love.

We told you we would be real with you—and the question everyone wants to know is, "*Where is the line when it comes to relationships before marriage?*"

But if true love calls us never to use the other person—if it calls us to put his or her objective good above our own desires, then this is the wrong question. It is sort of like saying, "How much can I take from this person before I cross over into using them?"

Here is the challenging truth we shared with our *Środowisko* students in Florence (and which we have shared with countless others): a love informed by the Gospel, which authentically measures up to the dignity of the person, means that *anything aimed at the arousal of the other is reserved for marriage.*

If we want a "line," that's where it is.

To be frank, we can offer a few concrete principles:

- *If an orgasm occurs, things have definitely gone too far.*
- *If either person is tempted to masturbate afterward (in effect, to "finish" what was started), things have gone too far.*[48]

- *To use an analogy: If you have no intention of going on a "road trip," then it is not wise—or in any way loving—to start the car and rev the engine.*

But what exactly qualifies as "revving the engine"?

This is something a couple eventually needs to discuss; but it will certainly include touching and caressing certain parts of the body—and it will likely include some forms of kissing.

At some point, a man will need to be honest with the woman because there can easily be confusion and miscommunication here. For example, as the relationship matures, what the woman may perceive as non-sexual affection can become a source of arousal and temptation for the man. A woman needs to be aware of this dynamic, and the man needs to be honest with her (where and when appropriate). This is especially true for a man who is striving for purity, for it will take far less for him to be aroused than she will likely expect.

HOW DO I WIN THIS BATTLE?

Chastity is a battle that no one wins by accident. It begins in the interior of the heart, and it is lost many steps before the fall actually occurs. Here are six keys that make for success:

1) *We must believe it really is possible to win this battle.* Many who struggle with pornography and masturbation do not really believe victory is attainable here. Part of this stems from the fact that few share their success stories with others, often because they don't want to appear boastful or make others feel bad who are struggling. While people need to hear that many others have these same struggles (and that they are not alone), they also need to hear inspiring stories of victory and success from those who have also struggled in this area and have overcome.

Stories of struggle and success need to be shared by both men and women, since both sexes struggle in this way.[49] For many women, their shame is compounded when they are made to feel like they struggle with a "guy" problem, which they often deal with in secret due to their shame and embarrassment.

2) *We have to really want this victory.* St. Augustine's quip looking back at his conversion in the fourth century still rings true today: "I had prayed to you for chastity and said, 'Give me chastity ... *but not yet.'*"[50]

No progress is made until we *really* want it. If we want it only halfway, then we have already lost. This is the distinction between *lukewarmness* and *sincerely striving* we have noted previously.

3) *We have to know our weakness and trust in the Lord.* This requires humility and patience, both with ourselves and with God. Sometimes the Lord helps us not in conquering a particular vice *immediately*, but by giving us the grace to continue trying, even after repeated failures. When we fall, we come face-to-face with our weakness, and this teaches us not to depend solely on ourselves—but upon the Lord.

C.S. Lewis captures this dynamic well, when he says that this "cures us of our illusions about ourselves and teaches us to depend on God. We learn, on the one hand, that we cannot trust ourselves even in our best moments, and, on the other hand, that we need not despair even in our worst, for our failures are forgiven."[51]

There is a powerful (even paradoxical) combination at play here: we need both a *relentless effort on our part* and *an absolute reliance upon God's grace.*

As various saints and writers have put it over the years, we need to "*pray as if everything depends upon God*; and *work* as if everything depends on us."[52]

4) *We have to be committed to avoiding the near occasions of sin.* This is part of what it means to acknowledge our weakness—and not overestimate our strength. As we have said, this battle is won many steps before the fall. As an old priest friend once put it: "Don't get mad that you didn't wake up to your alarm clock—get mad that you didn't go to bed on time."

If certain apps on your phone lead to problems with purity, delete them, or use them only in public settings. Make use of filtering or accountability apps. While these steps might seem drastic, the peace and joy that come from living a life of transparency are more than worth it.

For a couple, this means giving serious consideration to "trigger" situations that are near occasions of sin. For example, lying down on a couch together might seem innocent but can easily lead to a place of "no return." It is so easy to overestimate our strength, even with the best of intentions.

Young adults will often ask, "What did you do? Did you guys ever struggle here?" Yes, we know these temptations well. While we did not have sex until our wedding night, our journey was not perfect. The more we fell in love, the more we experienced very powerfully the fact that our *bodies wanted to follow our hearts.*

As many know, this is a slippery slope. Once a fall happens, the second one is not far behind—and boundaries tend to get pushed a little further each time. Eventually, about a year from our wedding day, we realized that we needed a plan, even if it included drastic measures.

We talked and prayed about it. We decided not to kiss or lie down together (for example, on a couch while watching a movie) again until our wedding day.

By this point, we had already kissed. We realized, however, that if we were going to win the battle of chastity, then we had to avoid putting ourselves anywhere close to compromised situations. We were sincerely committed to authentic love and the holiness of the other person—and it was clear that kissing and lying down together had become our "triggers."

While we obviously weren't perfect beforehand, we didn't kiss or lie down together for the whole year leading up to our wedding day. Because of that decision—and probably only because of that decision—we did not have another fall before our wedding day.

Was this hard, even somewhat strange, given that we had already kissed before?

Yes, of course.

But was it worth it and did it have a profound impact upon the development of our relationship and our preparation for marriage?

Absolutely.

And did those sacrifices make the wedding night unbelievably more incredible than it would have been otherwise?

Definitely!

If we are serious about chastity as a goal, we must be serious about the necessary *means* to this goal—the intermediate steps that are essential to making it happen. There is no other way. If we are not serious about the means, then we are not really that serious about the goal.

When interviewed, college football coach Nick Saban has said that one cannot focus only on the end—for him, winning a national championship—because there are parts of this outcome that are out of your control. But you can always focus on the *means*, the steps it will take to get there, because these *are* in your control.

The difference between winning and losing with chastity has everything to do with how serious we are about the steps that either put us on the road to success or bring us to the "triggers" that lead to our downfall.

We learned this the hard way, since for a time we thought we were serious about the "end," yet we allowed ourselves to wander down a slippery slope. We are so thankful we eventually learned this lesson, even though it was humbling. But being humbled is exactly what often brings us to our knees in prayer, renewing our zeal to do it the right way. This was definitely our experience.

5) *We need to be attentive to what is flowing in downstream.* We need to be attentive to what is shaping our minds and hearts. We are constantly receiving a bombardment from the world—images, billboards, music, movies, shows, conversations, social media, books, commercials, etc.—that subtly shape our perception of the good, that claim to tell us what beauty, love, and happiness should look like. Not only our minds but our hearts are constantly being shaped and affected by what we take in.

To use a visual image, imagine our souls as a lake, with various streams flowing into it. It will be nearly impossible to keep this lake clean if what's flowing in downstream is dirty—this is true *even if only one stream flowing in is dirty.*

If we are serious about chastity, we need to be attentive to what is shaping our minds and hearts.

Andrew: This came home for me in a powerful way as I was reading to our kids. I distinctly remember reading the Chronicles of Narnia when our older boys were around seven or eight. I had never read the Chronicles before, so I didn't know the details of the story. As we were reading *The Magician's Nephew,* we met "Uncle Andrew." One can hear a rank moral relativism (seemingly inspired by the philosopher Friedrich Nietzsche) coming out of Uncle Andrew's mouth when he says that moral laws don't apply to the likes of him:

> Rules of that sort, however excellent they may be for little boys— and servants—and women—and even people in general, can't be expected to apply to profound students and great thinkers and sages. No, Digory. Men like me who possess hidden wisdom are free from common rules ...[53]

Our older boys quickly developed an intense dislike for Uncle Andrew, even blurting out: "I hate Uncle Andrew!" At the time, I encouraged them to "wait and see" what happened in the story to see how his character would develop.

What dawned on me later was the *power of story* to teach about right and wrong in such a compelling way. Stories such as Narnia are so powerful because they show evil for what it is—ugly, wicked, and not something to emulate. Some characters, such as Edmund and Eustace, are transformed, going from ugly and wicked to noble and heroic. There are plenty of virtuous characters as well, clearly presented in a way that invites the reader to see them as heroic and worthy of emulation.

The point in all this is if we truly want our transformation and conversion to take full effect, *we have to tend to the formation of our hearts*. We have to pay attention to what we are letting in from the outside—and remove what poisons us with a distorted view of reality. We need to embrace what inclines our hearts more readily to the true, good, and beautiful.

As we like to say, *"If you want something to grow in your life, feed it. If you want something to die in your life, starve it."*

6) *We need accountability partners and support.* We simply can't fight this battle alone. We need people close to us, with whom we can be completely vulnerable and who will also check in on us and hold us accountable. Earlier we mentioned a group of young men who decided to fast twenty-four hours for each other whenever any of them fell sexually. This is a heroic example of accountability and solidarity. Just *knowing* that you are going to have to tell your closest friends about what happened—and knowing what that will require of them (fasting in the example here)—is already a powerful motivation to resist temptation in the moment.

You can make this your own—whatever helps you support and accompany one another.

To recap, the six keys to success in chastity are:

1. *Believe victory is possible.*

2. *Truly want this victory.*

3. *Know our weakness and trust in the Lord.*

4. *Avoid the near occasions of sin.*

5. *Watch what is flowing in "downstream."*

6. *Have accountability partners.*

In addition, a topic we will discuss more thoroughly later on is prayer. To really live out chastity, one needs the clarity and strength that only comes from intentional time spent with our Lord.

Chastity is the virtue that makes authentic love possible. While it is not easy, sincerely striving to live chastity is transformative. Even if you are not currently in a relationship, you are fighting for your future spouse and children.

We have to be committed to this as couples and as individuals. We can't just "try not to fall." We have to take seriously the above six steps—the intermediate steps—that make success possible.

It may seem overwhelming and daunting, but with God's help, you will be amazed at what you can do. With each small victory, you will find a snowball of momentum accumulating over time. In truth, you will be surprised at how far we can climb—by relying totally on God's grace and sincerely striving to make this happen. This is the explosive combination that makes for success—trusting entirely upon the Lord and striving with all you've got.

Yes, chastity is difficult; yet it is crucial. It really is one of the most important battles we face, because it is something that tests our character every day.

Sarah: I can honestly say that watching Swaff fight the battle of purity was one of the reasons I fell in love with him. I remember listening to him and his guy friends talk about the importance of getting rid of anything that stood in the way of their purity, and I remember watching them grow in friendship and brotherhood as they would hold each other accountable. I also clearly remember all times he would fight for me—and for us. Throughout our dating and engagement, he would lead. He would try to think one (or even ten!) steps ahead and put us in a place to succeed. He was creative, sensitive, and sacrificial.

Were we perfect? No. But we were striving, and we were in it together. And you know what? The virtue, holiness, and sacrificial love I saw in

Swaff when we were dating and engaged only made me love him more—and it is that same virtue, holiness, and sacrificial love that I have watched him grow in every day of our marriage. He continues to fight for me and our children. And it is beautiful.

The battle for chastity is a training in *self-mastery*. And self-mastery is the precondition for being able to give ourselves away in love—to make a complete gift of our lives.

We did not want to use each other, and we knew sinning together sexually hurt our relationship and each other. We wanted to elevate the virtue and holiness of the other, even when in the moment our bodies desired something else. We loved each other and wanted to show it, but we knew that the sacrifice of waiting until marriage and the swearing of our vows would be the ultimate expression of our love for each other. This took serious *grit*, but it was so worth it.

We tell you this because we do not pretend this is easy. Remember that it doesn't matter where you have been. *All that matters is where you are going.*

PART V

LIVING GIFT AND GRIT IN RELATIONSHIP WITH GOD

CHAPTER 12

WHAT DOES SEX HAVE TO DO WITH THE SPIRITUAL LIFE?

In this final part of the book, we will focus on living out meaning and grit as it relates to our relationship with God. *Yet here we are talking about sex again!*

Some people might think that sex and the spiritual life have little to no connection, but this simply isn't true. How we think about sex (and sexual sin) affects so much of our lives—and it can be one of the main things that keeps people from the Lord.

On the one hand, sexual matters are often a powerful example of forbidden fruit—something we desire strongly but in ways we shouldn't. After all, when we think of *temptation*, what comes to mind? Isn't the connotation of the word often somewhat sexual?

There is a reason for this. Sexual temptation in one form or another may be the most pervasive temptation we face every day, which is why authentic chastity is so crucial for a life of faith and virtue.

On the other hand, when we commit a sexual sin, the shame we experience can be so profound that we can come to see ourselves as unlovable and unforgivable, even by the Lord.

In Hebrew, the word "*Satan*" means "to accuse." In temptation, the Evil One poses as our "buddy," encouraging us to sin. But once we actually sin, he becomes the *accuser*, seeking to douse us in shame.[54] His great lie is that we are now too deep in our sin to ever come back out. And he will use our shame relentlessly to keep us buried there.

The Christian life is a paradox. While we are called to be "perfect" (Matthew 5:48) and conformed to the image of Christ (Romans 8:29), what Pope Francis once said is also true: "God never tires of forgiving us; *we are the ones who tire of seeking his mercy.*"[55] No one is ever too far gone. Rejecting Satan's lies, especially when it comes to sex, and believing in the reality and depth of God's mercy are paramount in the spiritual life.

The shame that the Evil One stirs up in our hearts can be like a dark cloud, creating an impasse between us and the Lord. While this covering remains, we cannot fully experience God's love—we can't fully experience his penetrating gaze. When we reject Satan's lies, however, the rays of divine love can once again pierce our hearts.

When we struggle to believe we are worthy of love, we should remember that God first loves us *not because we are good*—but *because he is Good* (see 1 John 4:10).[56] Right before receiving the Holy Eucharist, we say, "Lord, I am not worthy that you should enter under my roof. But only say the word and my soul shall be healed."

None of us are worthy. *But God makes us worthy.*

Our trust is in the power of God's word, which makes all things new, including us. The question is, *Do we trust him?*

WHEN OUR DEFENSES ARE DOWN
The battle for chastity is not easy when our spiritual vitality is high, but it is incredibly more difficult when our spiritual defenses are weak. The helpful acronym *B.L.A.S.T.* captures precisely when we are most vulnerable:

• Bored
• Lonely

- Angry
- Sad
- Tired

In these low moments, we experience a lapse in our spiritual strength, making it easy for us to resort to sexual outlets as a sort of "pick-me-up." But when we fail at chastity, our spirits are brought low, compounding our melancholy state. In fact, according to one psychologist—giving in to every sexual desire that comes our way is the fastest way to destroy our self-esteem.[57]

After all, do we ever feel really good about ourselves afterward?

SLOTH—THE VICE OF OUR TIME

While many think of sloth as merely laziness, this is only partly true. The Greek word for sloth is *akedia* (in Latin, *acedia*), which means "lack of care." As a deadly sin, it means "lack of care" especially regarding our spiritual life. Sloth is basically lethargy about the highest and most important things. It is *spiritual* laziness.[58] Jesus tells us to seek first the kingdom of God (see Matthew 6:33), and sloth yawns and says, "Maybe some other time." Sloth leaves us with a distaste for the things of God and saps our love, especially for the things that matter most (see CCC 2094).

As we have seen repeatedly, the most important thing we can do to grow in faith and virtue is to *live on mission*—as individuals, with friends, and as couples. This is what *Środowisko* is all about. Countless vices are overcome this way, with the support of friends, living on mission alongside one another—as they find a whole new sense of peace, joy, confidence, and freedom together.

In truth, sloth is the opposite of living on mission—the antithesis of living with meaning and grit. When we suffer from sloth, we feel as though we have lost our way, and it results in a certain sadness. In fact, Catholic tradition defines sloth as "sorrow at the difficulty of a spiritual good."[59] Hence, sadness is intrinsic to this vice.

Sloth is kind of like New Year's resolutions. We are excited about them ... until around February. At that point, the resolutions just seem too hard for us to sustain, leaving us sad and disappointed with ourselves.

The person suffering from sloth wants to be great, but the mountain just seems too high to climb—exactly how people often feel about chastity, as a nice aspiration but too difficult to actually live out.

If you are wondering if you have ever struggled with sloth, or if perhaps you are struggling with it right now, start with this question: *Have you ever found yourself bored with life, restless, or unfulfilled?*

It would be hard to find a person who hasn't struggled in this way at one time or another. This is the spiritual ache of our time—the pain of a life without meaning or purpose, which results in a loss of grit, as we just "float" along in life, unhappy and unfulfilled.

When we experience this, we inevitably look for ways to cope, as we try to *numb* our pain. We look for outlets, such as:

- *Pleasure.* This "comfort food" could be food, but it might also be pornography, sex, drugs, or drunkenness. To paraphrase St. Thomas Aquinas, man cannot live without pleasure; and if we can't find it spiritually, we'll look for it physically.[60] Pleasure can become a quick "Band-Aid" to numb and soothe our spiritual ache and boredom.

- *Entertainment.* Another way we often deal with sloth is simply to entertain ourselves. If we are suffering from sloth, we avoid quiet, reflective moments because we don't want to be alone with our thoughts. This may be manifest in an obsession with the twenty-four-hour news cycle or following sports in a compulsive fashion. Here is especially where social media can so easily consume so much of our lives—with endless scrolling and watching of videos, soaking up every spare minute we have.

- *Workaholism.* The fact that one can become a "workaholic" and still suffer from sloth shows that sloth is not synonymous with laziness, pure and simple.

We will consider the workaholic outlet further below, after we turn first to social media and its connection to our life of faith.

While we are certainly not anti-social-media or anti-screens in the Swafford household, we do recognize the power of technology. *Andrew:* For several years, I have assigned a forty-eight-hour tech fast to the students in my moral theology class. They can make and receive phone calls, but they cannot text or use social media. They can send and receive school or work emails, but they cannot surf the web, nor can they watch television, movies, or the like.

Naturally, they complain when they first hear about the assignment. But their reflection papers over the years have been eye opening. Consistently, they report:

- *reduced anxiety*
- *better sleep*
- *better conversations*

They also comment how much everyone else is on their phones (e.g., while standing in line for coffee).

They typically acknowledge how challenging the second day of the fast was. Sometimes they express shock at how much additional time they gained. For example, one student commented that she used to love to draw when she was younger but never had time anymore. During my tech fast, she found herself with a few additional hours—which she then spent drawing. She wistfully described how refreshing this experience was and how she had forgotten how much she had missed it.

Others had similar experiences, noting how much faster they got their schoolwork done—and how they even found time to read for pleasure, something which they had not done for a long time and really enjoyed doing again. They also recounted how much more time they had with friends and how much more relaxed they were overall. They often thank me for making them do this assignment—and often say that they hope to do a similar fast on their own in the future.

This experience of occasionally unplugging helps us tune in to what matters most. It helps us reflect upon the fundamental human questions such as *Who am I?* and *Where am I going?*

Andrew: When I have a student who is struggling with his or her faith, I often ask, "When was the last time you went outside at night and just looked up at the stars?" So often, especially when social media consumes all our "spare" moments, we end up suffocating the awe and wonder we once had as a child.

Awe at the transcendent beauty and wonder of creation is crucial for our faith. When we do not have any quiet moments for prayer, reflection, and wonder, we choke off our faith life (whether we realize or not). In our experience, one of the chief causes of secularization and loss of faith is the sheer busyness—the frenetic pace—of modern life.

Sarah: I have to take breaks, which I call my "holy smoke breaks." No, I don't actually smoke, but sometimes I just need to step out, catch my breath, reorient my heart and mind, and say a quick prayer. As a firstborn, choleric-sanguine *doer*, I have to stop and remind myself to just *be* for a moment and be grateful for the good and beautiful things in my life—just to take it all in.

If all we can think about is getting through the day, how is our life of faith ever to grow? Our interior life doesn't just stay stagnant when it's unable to grow—it eventually withers and dies.

As mentioned earlier, the third outlet for coping with sloth is to become a *workaholic*.

Sloth cannot be identified simply as laziness, because it can be present alongside a lifestyle of intense busyness. As with entertainment, busyness can be a way to numb the deep sadness and ache within our hearts. We do not want to be alone with our thoughts, so we fill our space with hyperproductivity. Deep down, we are yearning for meaning and purpose, but sloth makes us feel the hollowness of our lives—and we look to work to fill the void.[61]

This workaholic mentality can also include things like worshipping at the altar of the mirror. While working out is certainly a good thing for your health, when it becomes obsessive—especially over how we look—this can be just another mask we employ to hide the deep spiritual sadness of sloth underneath.

Engaging the deadly disease and vice of sloth by retrieving our sense of meaning and purpose—our meaning and grit—is crucial for the spiritual life. So often, sloth leads to difficulties with chastity—and failures in chastity in turn lead to deep shame, which saps our motivation for the spiritual life. For this reason, chastity is absolutely vital to the spiritual life, as failures here undermine our efforts in more ways than one.

A HEALTHY FEAR OF HELL

Certainly, there is more to the spiritual life than simply avoiding hell. After all, as St. Paul tells us, we are running to *win*, not simply to avoid losing (see 1 Corinthians 9:24–27). Nonetheless, a healthy fear of hell (along with a sense of grave or mortal sin) greatly helps us sustain the spiritual life. In our experience, this is also key to fighting the battle of purity—not only for ourselves, but also for those we are trying to love.

If love is willing the good of the other, then the most mature love is one that wills the greatest good for the other—namely, God himself. Therefore, *any action that takes someone away from this ultimate end can never be an act of real love*—no matter how "loving" it might feel.

If we have an authentic fear of hell and of committing a mortal sin, we could never encourage someone we love to commit such a sin with us—without experiencing tremendous pain and anguish immediately afterward. Something can never be an act of love if it jeopardizes the other person's eternal salvation.

It is Jesus who teaches us about hell more than anyone else (see, for example, Matthew 5:27–30; 13:40–42; 25:41–46). If we take our relationship with Jesus seriously, then we have to take his words on hell seriously. This is why hell has always been an integral part of Catholic teaching (see CCC 1035). While God truly is all-loving and all-merciful, he respects our freedom, even our freedom to reject him—and we can do so by our actions in this life.[62]

In mortal sin, God doesn't stop loving us; rather, *we stop loving him*. We place a block between ourselves and the supernatural gift of his life. In the end, what jeopardizes our salvation is *unrepentant* mortal sin. Taking mortal sin seriously means we have an urgency in seeking out the sacrament of Reconciliation after it occurs, and that we have a zeal to avoid the situations that easily lead us (or those we love) into it.

In other words, we have to be alert to the dangers of becoming lukewarm and indifferent to the reality of grave sin. If we get used to sin and lose our zeal for daily conversion (as with sloth), we cannot consider ourselves truly repentant. The slothful person is just being lulled to sleep spiritually. And in the area of sins against chastity, we can so easily fall prey to lukewarmness and various forms of rationalization.

C.S. Lewis captures this dynamic well when he writes: "Indeed the safest road to hell is the gradual one—the gentle slope, soft underfoot, without sudden turnings, *without milestones, without signposts*."[63]

STRIVING, NOT PERFECT
It is worth recalling what we said earlier about the difference between a person sincerely striving for holiness and the person who has become lukewarm or indifferent. Our journey here may not be perfect. Ours certainly wasn't. *What matters is that we are sincerely striving*—that we sincerely *want* to do it the right way. Someone who is sincerely striving and has a fall is very different from the person who has gotten used to sin

and become indifferent to it. The person sincerely striving to be virtuous makes frequent use of the sacrament of Reconciliation, with a firm resolve to change. He or she might not be perfect but perseveres in continuing to return to the throne of God's mercy, again and again.

Similarly, the person who has had a sexual past and now has a firm resolve to live differently often exhibits profound heroism. *No one is defined by his or her past.* No one is "damaged" goods. We must emphatically reject the lies of Satan, "the accuser," who seeks to bury us in the shame of our past.

Andrew: In a real way, I feel like I have been two different people—the "me" before my conversion, and the "me" after my conversion. Feeling like "my old self" has truly died has helped me heal from my past and forgive myself—through experiencing God's forgiveness. Like so many others, I have experienced the power of Christ setting me free.

When it comes to young people and their deep desire for a great love, our own experience matches that of St. John Paul II:

> After all, young people are always searching for the beauty in love. They want their love to be beautiful. *If they give in to weakness ... in the depths of their hearts, they still desire a beautiful and pure love ....* Ultimately, they know that only God can give them this love. As a result, they are willing to follow Christ, without caring about the sacrifices this may entail.[64]

Striving—not perfection—is what matters. If we sincerely want it, God's grace will see us through. He will make something beautiful out of us, no matter where we have been. He will even transform the sins of our past into powerful zeal moving forward.

As much as we might sometimes wish it were otherwise, there really is a direct connection between chastity and our spiritual health. While getting chastity right is not the only goal of the spiritual life, *it is often the precondition for getting everything else right*. When we live this out heroically, the rest of our spiritual life tends to fall into place.

A great many have experienced the pain of the other side—the pain of sexual addiction and the brokenness of promiscuity.

What if we tried it another way, with Christ as our guide from beginning to end?

Sincerely striving, with God's grace, can make all the difference.

We sometimes joke that sloth is our "favorite" deadly sin. It seems to be at the core of the deep emptiness people feel today, which leads so often to an attempt to numb our pain in self-destructive ways. As sloth leads to sexual sin, this only makes us feel worse about ourselves, as we feel even more unworthy of God's love and just want to give up.

Calling out the Evil One's lies and seeing his tactics clearly gives us great awareness and power to fight back. No more walking through life in a fog—the only real answer is to push all our "chips" into the middle of the table and go *all in* with the Lord.

WHAT DOES IT MEAN TO GO *ALL IN* WITH THE LORD?

Sarah: In high school, I went with some friends to a Christian rock concert, dc Talk for any fans out there. And if you don't know dc Talk, one of its founding members is TobyMac; and if you don't know who he is, just know that he is pretty cool.

At the concert, I saw a guy with a T-shirt that said, "Hey you!" on the front. As he passed by me, I turned around and read the back of his shirt, which said, "I'm into Jesus." I remember thinking to myself, "Poor guy, I bet he doesn't have many friends."

I know that was rude of me to think, but at the time, I couldn't have imagined being so publicly explicit about my relationship with our Lord. To be honest, that shirt haunted me for months. Then, one day, the Lord's gentle question became very clear to me: "Sarah, are you afraid to be seen with me?" The answer at the time was yes. And over the years I would discover that not only was I afraid to be seen *with* him, I was also afraid to truly be seen *by* him.

Like us, you may have struggled with the question, "What happens if I really go 'all in' with the Lord? If I really hand *everything* over to him, will I become something that I am not? Will I become someone that I am not? *Will I lose who I am?*"

It is like the story of the rich young man who comes to Jesus, asking how to inherit eternal life (see Matthew 19:16–22). Basically, he is asking, "What is it all about? What is the meaning of life?"

Jesus, of course, mentions the Ten Commandments, and the rich young man more or less responds, "Yeah, I have kept those pretty well." Basically, he is saying that he has always been a "good guy."

Yet he is coming to Jesus because he senses there must be something more. He feels that there is something missing in his life, even though he has kept the commandments.

Jesus, in effect, says, "You are right, there is more." Jesus famously exhorts him to give up what he has and come follow him. The rich young man then departs in sadness, unwilling to part with his many possessions.

This is a great story for all of us because there are many kinds of riches—and many different things that we can become attached to and unwilling to part with. Maybe it is a group of friends we don't want to lose, with whom there would be tension if we went *all in* with Jesus.

Maybe it is a relationship that we know is not leading either of us closer to Christ, but we find it difficult to walk away.

Maybe it is a work environment that is toxic to our faith, but we so badly want to climb the professional ladder that we try to fit in at all costs.

Maybe it is a matter of trying to fit in with buddies or colleagues who are doing things that we know are poison to the moral and spiritual life.

Maybe it is the image we have worked so hard to perfect.

Maybe it is a sin we keep secret.

Maybe it is our sense of never being enough and feeling unworthy of God's love.

You can fill in your own examples. Like the rich young man in the Gospel, a lot of us are more comfortable just being a "good guy." Deep down, we are afraid to go all in.

The radical and liberating truth that people typically describe when they do go all in with Jesus is that they do not lose who they are but became *a greater and deeper version of who they always were.*

When all is said and done, going all in is the only thing that makes sense. If not, we are playing a game of pretend. While we don't want to *reject* Jesus, we don't want him to be Lord of our life either. We don't want him *that* close.

But a half-baked relationship with Jesus doesn't really make sense. That is what you do when you don't really want to have anything to do with someone but are just afraid to say so. It's like a relationship where you don't want to be seen in "public."

What kind of friendship is that?

So the question is: Are we willing to be seen *with* Jesus, and are we willing to be fully seen *by* him?

BUT THIS IS TERRIFYING

At this point, some might be drawn to a deeper relationship with Jesus but still find themselves within the grip of various people pulling them in a different direction. It is very difficult to change when we are around people who have expectations of who we are, especially when we have participated in destructive behaviors with them. Those of us who have had serious conversions need to continually remember what it was like when our life was balanced on the edge of a knife and how terrifying that was at the time.

This point in our conversion is incredibly scary because we can see so clearly that if we "jump," many things in our life will change. Many describe overcoming this last hurdle as finally *feeling free to be the person they always wanted to be.* They see that the qualities they like about themselves have only become more developed and secure. If you are in this position, know that you won't "lose yourself." Rather, you will become a more confident and more joyful version of who you always were.

What you "lose" is the "rat race" of chasing happiness in things that do not really matter; you get to surrender trying to live up to people's expectations who often don't really have your best interests at heart.

And in truth, instead of focusing so much on what we are afraid to *lose*, we should ask ourselves if we have given serious thought to what we will *gain*.

"BUT I'D RATHER KEEP THE FAITH ON TERMS I'M COMFORTABLE WITH—I'M STILL TERRIFIED"

Others find themselves "flirting" with the Faith, attending events and developing friendships within a faith community. Yet they hold something back; they prefer to have one foot in a life of faith and one foot "free" to do whatever might be appealing, popular, or convenient.

We see this all the time—with college students, young professionals, and adults. They have the reputation of being a good Catholic because they go to Mass and have friends in the Catholic sphere. But if they were to go *all in*, this might cause a disturbance. It might mean, for example, that they would:

- *have to eliminate their habit of drunkenness*
- *need to stop using the Lord's name in vain*
- *have to make Sunday Mass a priority (even when inconvenient)*
- *start tithing regularly*
- *need to try to understand the Church's sexual teachings and not simply cower in the presence of friends and family who view things differently*

All of this is scary and likely to make us stand out—even making us appear "divisive." And the last thing most of us want is to not fit in, especially with family, friends, and colleagues.

AM I BEING DIVISIVE?

The truth is that *mediocrity loves company*. In fact, it is mediocrity that stands in judgment of greatness—because those who choose to go all in indirectly and unintentionally become a spotlight, illumining those who would rather not do so.

This was hard for many of us during our conversions, as well as for our students in Florence. They had had life-changing conversion experiences, but their friends and family back home did not have these same experiences. When our students came back to campus, there was some tension with some of their old friends. Generally, this tension had little to do with what our Florence students were *saying* but with how they were now *living*. Our *Środowisko* students wanted to continue going *all in*, as they had begun to do in Florence. They had experienced this in such a life-giving way, with friendships that found a whole new depth, different from anything they had experienced before. But their friends back home didn't feel the need to change old habits and inevitably felt "judged" in the presence of those who did.

Going all in feels divisive because it often brings about a self-indictment internally in the hearts of those who would prefer to keep Jesus at a distance and continue doing as they please.

It is far more comfortable to do the "Catholic country club" thing—a lot like the rich young man of the Gospel. It is like saying, "Well, what I'm doing is so much better than where the culture is, so it can't be that bad; I'm basically a good guy." For example, it's not uncommon for practicing Catholics to think drunkenness is OK (or to insist that drunkenness is only problematic at blackout), or to justify sleeping with their significant other (or to assume everything is all right as long as they are not having intercourse). These are examples of compromised discipleship. This is true even if someone is going to Mass every Sunday (or even multiple times during the week).

External commitments to attending Mass and even praying the Rosary are no guarantee of going *all in* with the Lord. Sometimes these very things can make a person blind to their need for change and conversion, as if they were just punching their "salvation ticket."

Real holiness is never simply about "jumping over a bar" set by our culture (a bar which is often lying on the ground!). Holiness means going all in with Jesus, being convicted and committed with grit and love and making a gift of yourself and your life. It is about a holy fearlessness—answering first and foremost to the Holy Spirit and not stopping at the limits of what is considered "acceptable" and "respectable" by our peer groups or family.

ARE WE GOVERNED BY FEAR?

Are we willing to go out of our comfort zone and *be seen with Jesus?* Are we willing to be truly seen *by him?* Are we willing to be inconvenienced for the sake of the Gospel? And if not, *why not?* What is holding us back?

After all, it really takes no courage to stand up for virtue when it is popular and convenient. But it takes real guts to do so when the situation is reversed.

A professor at Princeton once asked his students if they would have opposed slavery if they were alive in the 1830s. Of course, all the students raised their hands, saying they would have been unabashed abolitionists.

He went on to say: I'll believe you if you can show me a time when you stood up for people who were marginalized on account of truth and justice, *which came at great personal cost to you*; which led to you being despised by the powerful, who then labeled you with ugly names; and which resulted in your loss of employment and graduate school opportunities.

The fact is—despite what we might say—a great many people would *not* have had the courage to oppose slavery back then, despite their insistence to the contrary.[65]

Are we willing to stand by the truth today, even when it is unpopular?

Are we willing to stand with Jesus, even when it means being despised by the powerful, being called nasty names, and appearing out of touch with a culture that demands conformity to its ideological agenda? For this, we'll need courage. We will need to tap into a strength that goes well beyond ourselves.

This is where *Środowisko* becomes so important. As we have seen, communism in Poland in the twentieth century espoused an official ideology of atheism and a sexual morality that was decidedly at odds with the Church. The young people that Karol Wojtyła reached out to were swept up in this culture, and they were afraid to go against the grain. If they were to go all in with the Lord, there would definitely be trouble. When Wojtyła took them out of the city into the mountains, they formed friendships rooted in faith and virtue for the first time, and they felt free to be themselves and grow in their faith together. This gave rise to incredible friendships and even marriages—as well as the conviction to resist the ideological pressures of communism.

Something similar happened in Florence with our students, and with countless others with whom we have shared this message. It is what can happen anywhere when people go *all in* and live on mission together, supporting one another and running fearlessly to Jesus together.

PRAYER—THE ONLY WAY TO OVERCOME FEAR

To really overcome the chains of fear, we have to come to know the living God in a personal way; we need to have a genuine encounter with Jesus.

Sarah: One time after I gave a talk, a young lady approached me in all sincerity, asking: "In your talk, you said to pray … But *how* do I pray?"

We often use the phrase "pray about it." But how often do we talk about *how to go about this* and *what it really means to pray*? We may have learned a few memorized prayers along the way, but how many of us have ever had real instruction and counsel on how to have a *conversation* with the Lord?

How many Catholics, even those who attend Mass weekly, could even speak to this experience?

The young lady's question above is a real question, but one which we seldom address directly.

Unfortunately, many Catholics—even those who frequent the sacraments—do not have sincere conversation with the Lord on a regular basis. Many are not even sure how to go about it or where to begin.

While there are many forms of prayer, there is something powerful about *mental prayer* that gets to the very heart of what praying and discipleship are all about. We have found that this form of prayer is pivotal in overcoming the fear of going all in with the Lord.

Mental prayer is *listening* prayer. It is about having a conversation with Jesus, where we intentionally listen to what he is saying to us in the present.

It's best done before the Blessed Sacrament, sitting in the presence of our Lord and speaking with him face-to-face. But it can also be done at home with Scripture or some other spiritual reading. The important thing is that one actively seeks to listen to the Lord's voice—sitting in gratitude, thanking him, and seeing yourself as he sees you—and asking him intensely personal questions such as:

- *Lord, how are you calling me to grow?*
- *How are you calling me to change?*
- *What in my life needs to be removed?*
- *Where in my life are you calling me to go deeper with you?*
- *What parts of my heart am I afraid to share with you?*
- *What in me needs to be healed and reconciled?*

We might begin our time of prayer with spiritual reading, but we have to be careful that it doesn't become merely an act of *studying*; we have to be careful not to read too much. We need *silence*, both internally and externally—and our internal silence really begins when we stop reading.

Spiritual reading can be a starting point, inviting the Lord to speak to us through the text. Read slowly and in small increments, maybe just a single paragraph or even less. Ask Jesus how these words apply to us in the present moment.

If this is new to you, perhaps begin with five minutes of silence—or five minutes of reading followed by five minutes of silence to reflect on what you have read. Then, increase this period of silence to ten minutes. As with anything else, we have to develop a *habit* of prayer. In the beginning, even a few minutes of silent prayer may seem like an eternity. Eventually, work your way up to fifteen or twenty minutes (or maybe even thirty) of silent, listening prayer.

While it is good to have a set time period for prayer so you don't simply stop praying the moment you no longer "feel" like it, it can also be fruitful *not* to have a set limit and just focus on our conversation with the Lord for as long or as short as it needs to be. That said, given the human inclination just to follow our moods, committing to a period of time is usually wise, especially in the beginning.

Here is what we promised our students in Florence: *If you spend fifteen or twenty minutes a day listening in silence to the Lord, your life will never be the same.*

The fact is one can live a double life while still going through the motions of vocal prayer (Rosary, Mass, even daily Mass). But *one cannot persist in mental prayer and serious sin.* The silence is just too loud—either we will stop sinning, or we will stop praying, but we cannot do both for very long.

For this reason, a powerful step in our conversion is to commit to consistent mental prayer.

Andrew: I first began to pray this way during my sophomore year of college, when my conversion was really starting to take root. At the time, I was still dating my girlfriend from high school. The more I sat in silence with our Lord before the Blessed Sacrament, the more undeniably certain I became of what I had to do.

With noise and distraction, I could easily drown out the Lord's knock on my heart. But when I prayed in silence, I heard it clearly, and I knew that I had to leave the relationship with my girlfriend. It was the final thing holding me back from going all in with Jesus—from the life I longed to live.

My prayer before the Blessed Sacrament was always, "Lord, give me the *wisdom* to know your will and the *strength* to follow it through." This is exactly what happened. That December of my sophomore year, I ended that relationship, and my life was never the same. Mental prayer not only gave me clarity about what I needed to do, but it also gave me the strength to do what I couldn't imagine doing just a few months earlier.

Praying consistently in this way goes a long way toward awakening our conscience in a profound way. If we are living a double life, we will feel this contradiction in our heart. We will find ourselves empowered to make decisions we couldn't have imagined before—such as removing ourselves from a life of sin and not worrying about what others may think of us.

This can be scary. But nothing is more liberating than coming to grips with the fact that we answer to Jesus Christ above all and that we are no longer held back by the tyranny of "public opinion"—pining for acceptance and approval on social media and being a slave to what our old friends or even family might think of us.

MAKING HEROIC VIRTUE A PRACTICAL REALITY

The key to heroic virtue—virtue with grit—is that it is not just generic and abstract.

For example, sometimes it is easy to *say* we put God first in our lives. But when we recognize that putting God first involves taking certain concrete actions—such as a commitment to prayer, virtue, and chastity—this commitment starts to have more teeth. When it becomes concrete and specific, virtue becomes *heroic*. This is virtue with grit.

The issue is having the courage to live out virtue when it becomes difficult—when it appears burdensome, unpopular, or downright inconvenient. We want to share with you four pillars that will keep your relationship with Christ secure and on track.

THE BIG FOUR

1. *Mental prayer*

As one friend once put it, "Prayer isn't good for your relationship with God. It *is* your relationship with God."

The key here is consistency. Our prayer appointment with the Lord needs to become a nonnegotiable, scheduled part of our day. As we have said, we can begin with five or ten minutes, with a goal of slowly working up to fifteen or twenty minutes. Slowly increasing this time is important because it takes a bit of time for us to settle our minds and get into the flow of prayer and really listen to the Lord's voice.

Our prayer will not always be riveting; there will be dry spells. But just like an athlete who finds his or her "second wind," the same is true in prayer. Like exercise, what is important is to stay the course and be consistent. If we do, our lives will never be the same; this type of prayer will give us the strength to do what we know we *should* but are having trouble doing on our own.

2. *Rejection of drunkenness*

Drunkenness has no place in the Christian life. St. Paul speaks of it as a sin that can exclude one from the kingdom of God (see Galatians 5:21). For this reason, the Church has long regarded it as a serious and grave sin.

When we willingly get drunk, we intentionally impair God's gift of our intellect and will. In doing so, we make a mockery of our human dignity—not to mention endangering the dignity of those around us, spiritually and physically.

We need to be clear on what drunkenness is. As we have mentioned, some people mistakenly believe that drunkenness only begins when one blacks out. This is one of the countless "loopholes" we are so good at claiming to find.

We recommend using the legal limit of alcohol intoxication as a barometer. In almost all states, this is a bodily alcohol concentration of 0.08%, which most people reach after only a few drinks (though this varies based on several factors, such as body type and how quickly or slowly drinks are consumed). The bottom line is that a serious disciple of Jesus—someone who has gone *all in*—should never set out planning to need a designated driver.[66] If we make the legal limit our benchmark—whether we are driving or not—we will steer clear of the sin of drunkenness.

Sarah: As I wrote in *Emotional Virtue*, "drunkenness equals drama."[67] Nothing good generally comes from it, and it often leads people into places they never would have gone otherwise—especially in sexual matters.

3.   *A rejection of underage drinking*

This can be a tough one for American college students, the vast majority of whom are younger than twenty-one. They wonder what the big deal is for them to have a drink or two.

In our experience working with college students for over fifteen years, a culture of underage drinking tends to cultivate a bastion of lukewarmness, with the envelope soon getting pushed toward drunkenness, with sexual sins quickly following.

Is saying no to underage drinking inconvenient?

Sure.

Might this seem "radical"?

No doubt.

But the question is *are we willing to be inconvenienced for the sake of the gospel or not?* And if not, why not? Might this be a sign that we have not yet gone *all in* with the Lord—that perhaps Jesus is not yet truly Lord of our entire life, which is why we are unwilling to be inconvenienced for his sake? One thing our experience clearly shows is this: those who are willing to be inconvenienced here for our Lord almost never lack for zeal in the spiritual life.

4. *Chastity*

If our dealings with alcohol and sex are rightly ordered (and we are praying), there is a good chance that the rest of our lives are falling into place as well.

As we have seen, chastity is a positive virtue that frees us to interact with the opposite sex for who they are and not simply what they can do for us. In this way, chastity liberates us from using one another and fosters true love.

Many will "nod" at the good of chastity and then assume they are living it out as long as they are not having sex—that is, not "going all the way." We have even encountered Catholic couples who spend the night with each other, thinking this is all right, as long as they are not having intercourse. This, however, widely misses the mark of what chastity is all about.

As we have noted, the specifics of heroic virtue when it comes to chastity mean that *anything aimed at the arousal of the other is reserved for marriage.* If there is a "line," this is it.

The only way to win at chastity is to know ourselves and not put ourselves in compromising situations. If we get too close to the fire, we're bound to get burned.

Are these four things difficult?

Absolutely.

We do not pretend for a moment that this does not involve serious sacrifice. But we would be lying to you if we said that these four pillars didn't really matter. In our experience, those who make these "big four" a priority do not struggle with being lukewarm—they are consistently zealous for growing in the spiritual life.

For us, living the Christian life only got exciting when we became really committed to it—when we went *all in*. Going halfway never really made sense. After all, what is the point of that, really?

What we offer here *is* radical … but it is undeniably transformative, both in our lives individually and in our relationships. Nothing else is ever the same. For us, it is like life really began when we took this step, and we have seen this same transformation in countless others.

Going all in with Jesus is not easy, but it's worth it. Everything worth having in life comes at a price, and the same is true here. At the end of the day, *discipleship that costs nothing means nothing.*

CHAPTER 14

I KNOW I NEED HEALING, BUT WHERE DO I BEGIN?

Sarah: Years ago, after speaking at a conference, I was hanging out by my booth and meeting young adults—one of my favorite things to do. A young woman approached me, and I could tell she had been crying. Somewhat shakily, she smiled at me, and as I reached out to hug her, she started sobbing. I let her cry, and eventually asked, "Are these happy tears or sad tears?" She pulled back and said, "Both." She then remarked, "You were right when you said, 'Hurt people hurt people.' But you know what, Sarah, *'Healed people heal people.'*"

When I was bullied in seventh grade, my mom would say, "Hurt people hurt people," as she explained that something must be deeply hurting in those girls for them to want to hurt me so badly. But the way this young lady put it added a certain twist, suggesting that it goes both ways: while hurt people hurt others, *healed people can help heal others.*

I used to ask God, "Why was I bullied? Why did *[fill in the blank]* happen to me? Why do I still struggle with *[fill in the blank]*?" But I have come to see that my own suffering and healing has made me very empathetic to others' pain because I have been there. I have a profound desire to help because I have been helped in so many ways. And I continue to experience healing, forgiveness, and restoration. This journey is lifelong.

"I AM THE LORD, YOUR HEALER" (EXODUS 15:26)

We love to remind people that God wants not only to forgive us but also to *heal* and *transform* us.

God's work in our lives is not complete merely with forgiveness, as important as that is. The cross and resurrection point to two aspects of the mystery of Christ—God's definitive dealing with sin (on the cross) and his gift of new life (in the resurrection) (see CCC 654).[68]

What happened to Jesus is exactly what God will do in each of us, as members of his Mystical Body, the Church. The Christian life is all about *sharing in the life of Christ*, which means each of us will go through the cross and each of us will be infused with the glory of his resurrection.

While this refers to our own resurrection of the body at the end of time, it also points to *God's desire to make us whole in the present—spiritually, psychologically,* and *emotionally.* This is all part of what our Lord came to do (and continues to do)—in transforming sin, death, and human dysfunction: he seeks to make all things new (see Revelation 21:5).

No one gets through life unscathed. Each of us has wounds that likely go back to our youth and childhood. Maybe we were bullied or left out at school. Maybe we felt like we could never be enough to please our parents. Maybe we repeatedly tried to reinvent ourselves to impress others. Maybe we were never able to truly appreciate our gifts and never able to fully accept our flaws and limitations.

Maybe we lost a parent or loved one at a tender age.

Maybe we were sexually assaulted or abused—or neglected, abandoned, and emotionally unattended to.

In whatever room we walk into, we can count on the fact that there are heavy stories and heavy hearts among us—stories of immense pain, suffering, and heartache.

The name *Jesus* means "God saves." He saves us from sin and death. And he seeks to heal us from all that ripples outward from there, including the human dysfunction that gives rise to so many of the heavy wounds we carry.

IS THIS JUST ABOUT SELF-HELP?

As we have already started to see, the importance of dealing with our wounds and seeking healing is not just about us. Whatever wounds we leave unattended will show up in some other way. In fact, unattended wounds will ultimately *hinder our ability to love.*

Whether we realize it or not, we deal with such unattended wounds in many ways, often by developing coping mechanisms, subtle ways of protecting ourselves—like keeping others at a distance and not letting them get too close. We may go years without ever realizing this, but our wounds cry out for healing. If not addressed, they will only continue to resurface in some way.

Therefore, the work of healing is never just about us. It is about removing the shackles that make it difficult for us to truly love—that make it difficult for us to get outside ourselves and let go of the relentless protection of our own egos. It is about becoming whole, so we can enter fully into relationships with peace and joy and experience their life-giving vitality— and become a source of life for others.

Our friends involved in healing ministries often put it this way: *Suffering that is not redeemed and transformed is simply transmitted.*[69]

Either we seek healing and become a source of life and grace for others, or we pass on to others the same dysfunction we have experienced.

In other words, others will suffer if we do not seek the healing we need. Certain habits of dysfunction are often repeated from one generation to the next—e.g., "My grandmother did this, so it passed on to my mother, which is why I do it as well."

This familial history may be the reason why we react to certain situations in particular ways. But we must never use this as an excuse for projecting this same dysfunction onto others, without making any attempt to heal and address it.

SELF-AWARENESS

Self-awareness—recognizing that there is a problem—is the first and most important step in initiating this healing process.

If nothing "bucks the trend," giving us a firm resolve to address the patterns we have experienced, then we may find ourselves repeating those same patterns with others.

But if we become aware of the dysfunction within our hearts—if we become aware that we act out of wounds from our past—then we take the first step toward healing and growth.

At this point, we begin to recognize our coping mechanisms for what they are. We start to see that what we have long thought to be "normal" may be far from it—and may not be a healthy way to interact with others. This self-awareness enables us to be open to what the Lord may want to show us and what he wants to do deep within our hearts—and through us, perhaps even in our families.

GOING DEEP

Self-awareness alone, however, is not enough. We cannot simply "fix ourselves" or will our own healing. The negative patterns in our life will not just go away on our command. Often, they require counseling.

It is not good to *spiritualize* every issue with which we struggle, for human beings are a body-soul composite. Some of our problems may be rooted in a lack of virtue and a need for a deeper prayer life, but many issues cannot be dealt with in only this way. We may need professional counseling and even prescription medication. Since we are a union of body and soul, we need to be attentive to all the different ways we may need healing—spiritually, emotionally, psychologically, and physiologically.[70]

It can help immensely to find a counselor who has a comprehensive vision of the human person—as a body-soul composite, made in the image and likeness of God. A counselor without such a view may be able to offer helpful tools and diagnoses, but his or her ability to help us will ultimately be limited.

THE POWER OF PRAYER

While counseling (and even medication) may be absolutely necessary, prayer remains vital for the Lord to bring about definitive healing in our lives. In our experience, the combination of sound counseling and a serious commitment to prayer is explosive in its transformative effect, often facilitating deep healing and newfound flourishing.

Prayer is like a slow and steady drip of water upon a rock, which over time causes it to erode and fade. It is like sitting in the sun for hours, which eventually alters our complexion. Prayer can be the Lord's "sandpaper," as he gently smooths out our rough edges. By placing ourselves in his presence (especially before the Blessed Sacrament) and inviting him deeply into our hearts, we are transformed in ways we cannot even fathom. This will take time, and we will not always feel its effects. Yet far more is going on in prayer (and the sacraments) than we can ever realize in the moment.

Sarah: When people ask me to share my testimony, I ask, "Which one? I have about eight different ones!" In other words, I can think of many occasions over the course of my life where the Lord has taken me deeper, where he has brought me across some new threshold—concerning something I was struggling with, something I was working on, or something I came to understand more deeply about my own journey and the particular wounds I carry. The Lord massages our hearts, addressing different layers within us. The longer we continue in the habit of prayer, the more we will see these different layers unfold before our eyes—and the more we will experience the *wholeness* and *newness* he desires to give us. This is where spiritual direction can also be very beneficial, giving us another person to help us discern the Lord's movement in our hearts.

Initially, maybe Jesus is just trying to pull us out of a life of sin in which we are stuck. Over time, though, he can help us see things in a more profound light, revealing some of the underlying reasons why we were perhaps so drawn to a particular vice. The Lord may help us see, for example, how certain wounds deep within us have inclined us toward various coping methods—e.g., sex, pornography, drunkenness, drugs, or gossip.

The Lord's work is about more than just getting us to stop sinning. He wants to heal and transform us. He wants to bring us into the fullness of life and joy (see John 10:10). He wants to *save* us in all these ways.

Through the sacraments and prayer, we come to recognize this reality ever more deeply. Especially here, we come to see ourselves as God sees us— as *broken*, *loved*, and *called to greatness*. We begin to see what he thinks matters most, and we begin to judge ourselves by his truth rather than by the "measuring stick" of the world.

Prayer is key for coming to grips with this and conforming our minds and hearts to the Lord. Prayer enables us to surrender to him all that we are— the good, the bad, and the ugly. In this way, prayer enables us to come to peace with who we are, helping us to accept the fact that we are both a *masterpiece* and a *work in progress*—recognizing that *God loves us just as we are* but *too much to leave us that way*.

Deep prayer helps us to see that our lives are no longer simply about "building ourselves up" with our own ambitions, plans, and accolades. Life is not about manipulating people and situations to get what we want. After all, so much of this can be just a defense mechanism, masking our insecurities, hurts, and wounds. In authentic prayer, there's no place to hide. We are emotionally "naked" before the Lord. In prayer—maybe for the first time—we are accepted as we are and simultaneously beckoned to become all that we long to be.

For all these reasons, embracing our deep need for healing and turning to Jesus, the Divine Physician, in prayer is *the* crucial step we must take to break away from the chains that have long held us down. Prayer (along with counseling and medication, if needed) brings us into a newfound peace, joy, and confidence—which the world simply cannot give.

As we come to know the Lord more deeply in the healing depth of prayer, *we come to truly know ourselves.*

While our wounds never totally vanish, the Lord begins to transform and integrate them into the glorious story he is writing in us, with us, and through us.

We are truly a sculpture that the Lord is fashioning from many different angles. Even our wounds and the traces of our sin—when transformed—become glorious aspects of what makes us who we are.

CHAPTER 15

HOW DO I DEAL
WITH MY PAIN?

One of the hardest things about the spiritual life is coming to grips with why bad things happen to us.

Andrew: When it comes to my relationship with my dad, I think "emotionally abusive" would be the way my two younger siblings and I would describe it. His schedule was dutifully arranged to avoid us. He generally chose to work second shift, which meant he wasn't there when we came home from school, and he was asleep when we left for school in the morning. When he was home, it was like having a stranger in the house—and it didn't take much to set him off. A misplaced television remote was more than enough to create quite the scene.

I have often wondered how this relationship with my father plays into my story, since it seemed to set me back in so many ways. I was never enough for him—no matter what, I could never attain his approval.

Where was the Lord in all these difficult times?

Long into my twenties, I still yearned for my father to be proud of me. I used to find ways to drop hints at what I was up to, especially regarding my accomplishments. But every time, he dismissed my "accomplishments" as not really being that significant—certainly not on par with those of others. For example, when I shared with him that I was learning Hebrew, his response was, "Well, it's probably not as difficult as Chinese."

This continued a trend begun in high school. Whenever I tried to share my athletic accomplishments or those of my team, his response was always the same: some other player or team was always superior to me or my teammates, no matter what we were able to do.

Eventually, I gave up. I realized that it was a fruitless exercise that was set up to fail—getting my hopes up, only to have them dashed each time. After my conversion to Christ, I realized that I did not need my father's approval. As much as I wanted it, I didn't *need* him to be proud of me—because I had encountered the love of my heavenly Father and I had *his* approval.

For much of my life, I placed my stock in what others thought of me, whether it was my father or certain friends. While we should care about what some people think (e.g., our mentors, the people we respect the most), there are many others to whom we subconsciously hand over the keys to our peace and joy. We might do this with friends or a significant other who is pulling us in a negative direction, whose opinion we have long cared too much about. Perhaps, as in my situation, it is a parent whose approval never seems to come. Life is too short to allow others to have such control over our lives—especially when it comes to our peace and joy.

SURRENDERING OUR PAST TO THE LORD

There are many things we will not fully understand on this side of heaven.

To heal and overcome the bitterness that may reside deep within our soul, we need to go back into the dark places of our past where we do not want to go—places where we have been hurt, places in our heart to which we have long bolted the door and kept it shut.

This hurt may have been at the hands of those who were supposed to love us—or who loved us very imperfectly. The memory is often so painful that we would rather not think about it. But what fundamentally transforms this suffering is going back there with Jesus and allowing him to redeem these moments. We cannot just "stuff" these memories and negative feelings. We have to bring them to Jesus and allow him into these closed quarters of our heart. We have to allow ourselves to be emotionally naked before the Lord, to be fully open with him. This is the path of true healing.

There is no other way. If we don't let the Lord in, we will eventually transfer this suffering to others in some other way, often in ways we don't see or intend.

Andrew: It is easy for me to assume that if I had a great father, I would have likewise become a great father to my own children. But maybe this is not exactly right. Perhaps I would have taken it for granted and become complacent in my own fatherhood. In prayer, I have come to realize that, in many ways, I am the father I am precisely because of what I didn't have growing up. In this way, over time, I have come to accept what the Lord allowed to be a part of my story—namely, my relationship with my father. I have even come to see the mysterious ways in which God's providence has been able to work through it.[71]

Yet, I never would have chosen it for myself.

Sarah: The same is true for me. I would never have chosen to be bullied, to lose my aunt, or almost lose my dad to cancer, to be cheated on, or the countless other pains I have experienced in life. But I can see how God has brought beauty, understanding, and empathy out of all of it.

This, however, is not to engage in a "moral calculus." It is not to say, "Aha! Now I see why all my sufferings were worth it." Rather, it is to acknowledge that what we see in our lives is like a single paragraph of a great novel—we could never understand the full meaning of our part in the story without knowing all the twists and turns that only the divine author can see. Only with the perspective of eternity—and a deep sense that *Christ suffers in us and with us*—do we begin to glimpse some meaning in our sufferings. Only then can we begin to realize that God has not forgotten us.

WHAT ABOUT FORGIVENESS?

None of this will ever be easy. It will take much time for the Lord to help us see it. But surrendering our past to him in trust helps tremendously in letting go of anger, resentment, and bitterness. It can even help us to take steps toward forgiveness deep within our hearts.

Importantly, forgiveness does *not* mean that we forget the past, nor that we no longer have strong feelings about it. And: *forgiveness does not necessarily include reconciliation.*

Forgiveness is about *surrendering our right to hold the other in our debt*—in effect, to *release* the debt of justice they truly owe us on account of the wrong they have done, a wrong which they likely can never repay. This means we no longer keep score.[72] We can do this whether they are sorry or not, precisely because forgiveness is often separate from reconciliation. The act of forgiveness is about *letting go of their debt.* It is more about *us* than it is about them, which is why it is always worth it, even when those who have hurt us are not sorry—even when there are no serious prospects of mending the relationship in sight.

This movement of forgiveness helps us focus on the present and not remain stuck in the past. It helps us surrender not only the future to the Lord, but the past as well—which can become a pivotal step forward in the healing process.

THE EXAMPLE OF WALTER CISZEK

In many ways, Walter Ciszek embodies everything we have been writing about, both in this chapter and throughout this book.

Walter Ciszek was born in Pennsylvania in 1904 to Polish immigrants. After a childhood of getting into a good bit of trouble and excelling as an athlete, he suddenly decided to enter the seminary and become a Jesuit priest, much to the surprise and dismay of his own family, especially his father.[73]

One day during his seminary training, in 1929, the rector read a letter from Pope Pius XI calling for missionaries to Russia, especially from the

Jesuit "sons of the Church." As the pope's letter was being read, Ciszek immediately felt that the Lord was speaking directly to him. He literally couldn't wait to be a missionary in Russia, despite the dangers involved in ministering to people under the grip of atheistic communism.

After his ordination, Fr. Ciszek was sent to Rome and trained to be a missionary, learning the Russian language, culture, and history. To his immense disappointment, however, his superiors deemed it too dangerous to send missionaries to Russia. Instead, he was sent to eastern Poland in 1938 to serve Catholics there.

As World War II broke out, the Russians invaded this area of Poland. Prior to this invasion, the American embassy in Warsaw reached out to Ciszek multiple times, strongly encouraging him to return to the United States. Each time, he declined, insisting that he needed to stay with his flock.[74]

Eventually, the Russian army took over his parish and the seminary there, making it impossible for Ciszek to continue his ministry.

At this time, Russia was actually accepting "volunteer" workers in the Ural Mountains to support the war effort. Ciszek and another priest (who also trained with him in Rome to be a missionary) saw this as their chance to fulfill their dream of becoming missionaries in Russia. Both adopted false names and fake life stories. Ciszek became "Walter Lypinski," a widower who lost his wife and three kids in a German air raid,[75] and the two crossed the border into Russia.

These two priests went undercover, doing grueling work for very little money, which was often barely enough to buy food. They couldn't tell anyone they were priests, as they tried to determine how they could carry out their ministry under such challenging circumstances.

This lasted about a year, until one night Ciszek was arrested at 3:00 AM and brought in for questioning. The Russian interrogator knew his entire life story—his real name, the fact that he was a Jesuit priest, the year of his birth, that he was born in Pennsylvania, *everything*. Since the communist officials could not possibly understand Ciszek's spiritual motives for being in the country, he was arrested as a German and Vatican spy.

He eventually served *fifteen years* in a Communist labor camp in Siberia, where the prisoners were worked to the bone, fed very little, and beaten endlessly. *But it was only there that Fr. Ciszek was finally able to exercise priestly ministry in Russia.*

What got Ciszek through this horrendous time is that he had an amazing trust in God's providence. Because of this trust in the Lord, he never lost his sense of *meaning* and purpose, even in a slave labor camp. If he was called to be a worker, that's what he did—and this became his prayer. When the other workers would ask him why he was working so hard, he responded that since the Lord had placed him there, his work would become his holy offering.

Amazingly, he never became bitter. He never expressed sorrow at "what could have been." He never regretted crossing the border into Russia.

Because of his deep sense of meaning and purpose, he had the supernatural *grit* to see God's will in the *concrete circumstances of his life*. For Ciszek, God's will was never "elsewhere"—it was right where he was, in the middle of a Communist slave labor camp. He couldn't change these circumstances, but he definitely (through God's grace) was in control of the lens through which he viewed them. Reflecting upon this experience, Ciszek later writes:

> We are not saved by doing our own will, but the will of the Father; *we do that not by interpreting it or reducing it to mean what we would like it to mean,* but by accepting it in its fullness, as made manifest to us by the situations and circumstances and persons his providence sends us. It is so simple and yet so difficult. Each day, and every minute of every day, is given to us by God with that in mind. *We for our part can accept and offer back to God every prayer, work, and suffering of the day, no matter how insignificant or unspectacular they may seem to us.* Yet it is precisely because our daily circumstances often seem so insignificant and unspectacular that we fail so often in this regard. ... Between God and the individual soul, however, there are no insignificant moments; this is the mystery of divine providence.[76]

Ciszek never lost his trust in God—and he came to see God's will as manifest in the day-to-day of his life, even in the midst of such tragic circumstances. He never lost his sense of meaning and purpose, as is evident here in his devotion to bringing our Blessed Lord in the Eucharist to his fellow prisoners:

> Our risk of discovery, of course, was greater in the barracks, because of the lack of privacy and the presence of informers. Most often, therefore, we said our daily Mass somewhere at the work site during the noon break ... The intensity of devotion of both priests and prisoners made up for everything; there were no altars, candles, bells, flowers, music, snow-white linens, stained glass, or the warmth that even the simplest parish church could offer. Yet in these primitive conditions, the Mass brought you closer to God than anyone might conceivably imagine ... So I never let a day pass without saying Mass; it was my primary concern each new day. *I would go to any length, suffer any inconvenience, run any risk to make the bread of life available to these men.*[77]

While we might never suffer in a slave labor camp, there is a powerful lesson here for us all, no matter our state of life. It all comes down to *meaning* and *grit*—receiving the meaning of our lives as a *gift* from the Lord, even when it is not the particular "gift" we would have chosen for ourselves.

Ciszek never tried to resist God's will as it was manifested in the concrete circumstances of his life, especially when he couldn't change those circumstances. Certainly, he never would have chosen this path for himself; but once it was presented to him as something he could not escape, he sought to unite his will with that of the Lord—accepting and embracing the path that the Lord had mysteriously woven into his story. And his relentless sense of meaning—his sense of divine mission from the Lord—enabled him to persevere through the most grueling of circumstances. He never lost his fundamental sense of purpose, and that's what got him through.

Sometimes the Lord allows bad things to happen and even weaves the evil choices of others into our story. Painful as this is, this is not a sign of God's weakness but his strength. The Lord is the great jiu jitsu artist, who turns evil against itself—even drawing good out of it. In fact, some goods are only possible when they are drawn forth from evil. For example, if there were no *tyrants*, we wouldn't have *martyrs*. Even though it doesn't always feel like it, evil will never have the last word.

Amazingly, Ciszek showed a complete *lack of resentment* toward the people who held him captive. In fact, as his plane was departing to return to the United States—after twenty-three total years in Russia— he looked out the window and blessed the land that had brutally abused him for so long.[78]

How he maintained his peace and joy through it all defies any natural explanation. This is the work of the Holy Spirit; this is a life brimming with divine meaning. This is what supernatural *grit* is all about.

MEMENTO MORI

There is an ancient saying, popular among the medieval friars— *memento mori*, which means "remember your death."[79] The saying is not meant to be morbid. Rather, it is about living in a way that we would be proud of *if we were to look back upon our lives from the vantage point of our deathbed.*

It's about living with eternity in mind.

Living with this perspective leads to a lot less regret and empowers us to have the grit to live out the burdensome and painful moments of life with peace and joy. We might not be in a concentration camp, but we will face moments of monotony, drudgery, and suffering. We will experience times when we seem to have lost our way.

What will carry us through in these moments?

What will give us peace and joy amid suffering and trial—or when our life just feels so mundane and unimportant?

Witold Pilecki (pronounced "Vee-told Pilets-kee") is another man who embodies *memento mori*. A Polish war hero of World War I, he was executed by the communists shortly after World War II, after being falsely accused of treason.

He is remembered for going to his death with these words: "I have tried to live my life in such a way that at the hour of my death I would feel *joy*, rather than *fear*."[80]

The Lord is doing a great work in each of us. But we only see through a glass darkly (see 1 Corinthians 13:12). By faith, we know that even the parts of our lives we consider ugly and dark are being woven into the tapestry of his providence.

It is the Evil One who wants us to cling to our past, with bitterness and shame.

The Lord wants us focused on the *present*—which is *where time and eternity kiss*. He sets us free from the chains of our past and is making something new and beautiful out of us as we speak.

We believe in the Lord's providence not because it is easy or we have all the answers but because we trust him. We trust that he is writing a beautiful and powerful story, in which we have a momentous part to play. This faith enables us to see our lives as *gift*, which empowers us with the grit to make a gift of our lives in return.

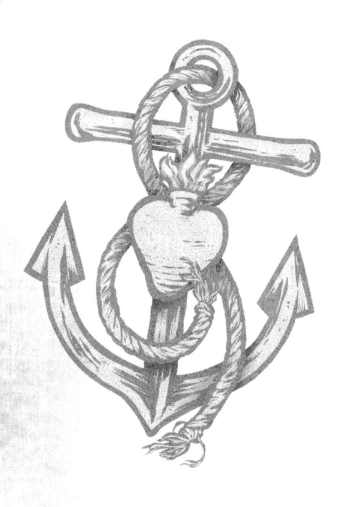

CHAPTER 16

HOW DO I LIVE WITH ETERNITY IN MIND?

We know that we have shared some hard truths with you in this book. Some of them will take you some time to wrestle with and pray through. It has taken us years to work through our own journeys of conversion and healing. And you know what? *We are never finished.* We will never be "done."

Perhaps the most important starting point is that a life of meaning and grit boils down to this: *our lives are not ultimately about us.*

So much of our sadness, bitterness, and resentment stem from forgetting this truth—leading to frustration and disappointment when we experience the absence of meaning in our lives.

When we turn inward, our lives become all about ourselves, and our sense of meaning is sapped. As our sense of meaning wanes, so too our grit.

We can get through an awful lot when we have a clear sense of meaning and purpose—when we have a clear sense of what our suffering is *for*. But when we lose our sense of meaning and purpose, it doesn't take much to knock us down.

Our deepest *why* comes from God—who has given us the gift of our lives and our calling, our vocation, to which we can give our lives in love. We have been loved into existence—we are called, chosen, and commissioned *for a time such as this* (see Esther 4:14). And discovering the unique part we are called to play in this great story is precisely what makes life so exciting.

WHAT IS THE ANCHOR OF OUR LIVES?

We all worship something. All of us have a matter of ultimate concern, which gives our lives meaning, purpose, and direction. This is what drives us to push forward each day.

Many of us want to say that God is number one in our lives. But in truth, *what we worship is best revealed by how we live.* It is especially revealed in how we spend our time, money, and emotional and psychological energy. If you want to see what you worship, consult your daily planner and your credit card statement.

What are the things we consistently make time *for*, things we simply won't skip? What are the things for which we rearrange our schedule? What are we constantly thinking about and getting excited about?

Are we willing to make time for the Lord in this way?

Where does prayer rank among our priorities?

Do we make time for important relationships, especially those with whom we are seeking to live on mission—our *Środowisko*?

In many ways, *time* is the most precious resource we have—and the things to which we give it are often a clear indication as to where our hearts lie.

The same is true with how we spend our money. This reveals what we value and where we put our trust.

DO WE REALLY NEED TO TITHE?

Everyone wants to hear Catholics talk about sex and money, right?! Not really. But both are so important and powerful that they can and will take over our lives if we are not careful.

There is a deep biblical tradition of *tithing* and *almsgiving*—of giving some of our money away. For Catholics, these are not "extras" but are staples of what it means to live a Christian life.

All that we have is God's. We are stewards, not owners, of the gift of our lives and everything we have. It is all his—and he lets us keep ninety percent. The reason for tithing is not because God needs it, but because we do—we need to detach from our addiction to the false security money purports to provide. Even if everybody's needs were met, all of the Church's finances were in order, and every charity and apostolate was fully supported, we would still need to give in order to rid ourselves of this attachment.

Tithing and almsgiving are ultimately about *our doing with less* so that those who have less can have a *chance*. There really is something to *living simply* so that others can *simply live*.

We are consistently told in Sacred Scripture not to "test" God (see Deuteronomy 6:16 and Psalm 95:7–11), but there is one notable exception—and it has to do with tithing: "Bring the full tithes into the storehouse, that there may be food in my house; *and thereby put me to the test*, says the LORD" (Malachi 3:10, emphasis added).

The question is: In whom or what do we place our trust?

When we were newly married in graduate school, there were moments when it wasn't clear how we were going to pay our bills. We had two young children, and our date nights consisted of going to the Olive Garden and sharing a single entrée (the "Tour of Italy" for those who are familiar)—and then asking for extra salad and breadsticks! This was a time when we did a lot of oatmeal for dinner.

While it was tempting to forgo tithing during this challenging financial time, the choice to continue doing so became a source of tremendous growth for us. It became a conscious decision not to think with the logic of the world—not to act as if God weren't real. It became a way for us to take the *risk* of faith.

In truth, taking such risks—as only someone who truly believes would do—is a powerful way to grow in our walk with the Lord.

When we risk our time and money in this manner, our faith grows in unique ways, and we are changed in the process. We made it through that tough season early in our marriage. We scraped by and sold whatever we could—but in truth, the math never did quite add up. We are not exactly sure how we made it through financially, but we did. He provided for us.

EVANGELIZATION—SHARING THE RICHES OF OUR FAITH

You might be thinking: "What does evangelization have to do with tithing or almsgiving?"

But like our time and financial resources, it is ultimately about stewardship, recognizing that our lives are not our own—everything is gift. This includes the gift of our faith. It is not ours to keep for ourselves.

Evangelization is about being a spiritual steward of the riches we have been given, riches that are not meant to stop with us.

Unfortunately, many people think of evangelization as simply an effort to get others to join our "party." But evangelization is *spiritual service*—it is about loving our neighbor.[81] It is about giving others the *greatest gift we could ever give them*, the gift of knowing Jesus Christ in this life and the next.

The Lord's missionary mandate to make disciples of all nations (see Matthew 28:19–20) is ultimately an expression and application of his call to love (see Matthew 5:43–44).

The real question is, *Do we sincerely believe in the truth of the Faith* and *truly love those around us?*

Our failure to evangelize often stems from a less-than-vigorous yes to this question. Either we are not fully convinced of the truth of the Faith, or we are not fully committed to loving our neighbors.

When all is said and done, evangelization not only offers others a most precious gift, it also grows our own faith. Indeed, evangelization is a great example of how in giving, we receive (see Acts 20:35).

That which we keep private—those things we keep to ourselves and never share publicly—tend to become less and less real in our minds and hearts, slowly eroding over time.

This happens to high school and college students, those in the workplace, and even to people in their own homes when the Faith goes so often unmentioned to the point where it almost ceases to be real. Sometimes people lose their faith in these settings not by an abrupt moment or argument but by a slow and steady absorption of their surroundings, often encouraged by their deep desire not to "rock the boat" and just fit in.

Conversely, *our faith grows when we share it.*

When we share our faith, we own it—and it becomes more and more real in our lives.

BUT HOW?

This might make sense but still feel incredibly intimidating. So how do we go about doing this? Are we just called to be "wrecking balls" for Jesus against our culture, perpetual wet blankets for our family and friends, putting a damper on everybody's fun?

To make sharing your faith more realistic and manageable, here are five tips that have proven immensely helpful and effective over the years.

I.   *Have the courage to be yourself.*

The first step is to just be yourself. This doesn't take much; you just need to find small ways to make the importance of your faith known to others. For example, when asked "How was your weekend?" on a Monday morning, instead of just saying "fine," perhaps talk about what you might have done that was related to your faith. Maybe you went to a talk or conference, or just had a really moving confession. Share a bit about that experience, just a sentence or two. If the person wants to ask more, he or she can.

There is nothing "in your face" about this. Over time, finding small ways to acknowledge the meaningfulness of your faith can move mountains. It invites future conversations and plants seeds for those around you. You will be surprised by the number of questions and conversations that will come your way, if only you have the courage to be yourself.

2. *Continue to feed your faith.*

There is a real sense in which neither the Catholic Faith nor any other idea will remain alive in our hearts *unless it is fed.*[82] We become what we repeatedly think about. As we have noted, it is easy to take on the attitudes of our surroundings. We need influence from another direction. If our faith means something to us, we need to feed it by prayer, Bible study, virtuous friendships, good books, talks, and podcasts, among other things. If we don't, our faith will slowly wane over time. As it becomes less and less real to us, it ceases to be at the forefront of our minds and hearts, and our evangelization efforts dry up.

In contrast, if we feed our faith and it is alive in our minds and hearts, it will come out naturally and organically—as an authentic expression of who we are.

3. *Don't be afraid to let people vent.*

If we have friends, family members, or coworkers who have strong feelings against the Church, we shouldn't be afraid to simply let them vent and hear them out. In other words, we should not get defensive. It is often disarming when we just listen to them, without getting upset. Nobody changes their mind about something they consider important in five minutes or even in one sitting—which means we have to play the long game. Our compassionate and sympathetic listening will disarm their anger and over time may earn us the right to be heard.

4. *Make the personal dimension of your faith known.*

This is like the first item but with a twist. When given the opportunity to share about our faith, we cannot simply hide behind apologetics and ideas, as important as these things are. Make sure you also make the personal dimension of your faith known—that is, *your personal relationship with the Lord.*

Research points to the fact that a person can only go so far in investigating the possibility of faith if they haven't come to believe that a *personal relationship with God is possible.*[83]

But where will they ever come to entertain this idea if we never give them a glimpse of our own personal relationship with the Lord? How will they ever entertain it as a possibility for themselves?

This takes vulnerability on our part. Where appropriate, we need to have the courage to do this. All the "perfect arguments" and apologetics in the world can only take us so far if we do not introduce people to a personal relationship with the Lord—and the best way to do this is to find ways to share our own experience with them.

   5. *Less is often more.*

Sometimes when the faith conversation finally comes up with friends or family, we are tempted to douse them with six months (or six years!) worth of information we have been dying to share with them. This almost never goes well.

We have to tread carefully here. We are better off simply planting seeds. We do not want to overwhelm their budding curiosity by sharing everything we have learned in one sitting. We often do best when we assume that we will get another chance. That way, we can temper how we approach the situation.

We do well to think more modestly about our endeavor—trying to help the person move "one level up," as it were. That way, we will not feel the weight of the world upon our shoulders, as we do when we try to go for the "home run" all at once. Typically, we make more progress incrementally—because when our goals are more modest, *we evangelize more often.* Whereas when we have an all-or-nothing approach, we get overwhelmed and often fail to even begin.

UNDENIABLE WITNESSES

There are a few things that even those who seem most closed off and indifferent to the Faith generally recognize as compelling witnesses. For example:

- *radical love for the poor and marginalized*
- *peace and joy amid suffering and trial*
- *uncompromising purity and chastity*
- *profound forgiveness*

We have to show the world *the difference that Jesus makes.* For if Christianity is just about being a "nice person," people can find that in lots of other places.

People need to see this difference in *us*—especially in how we handle suffering, service, money, and sex, as well as the sometimes incredibly difficult task of extending real forgiveness to those who have hurt us.

Our love for the poor is evidence that we know that this life is not the end—and the same is true of our peace and joy amid suffering. These are not *normal* human responses, which is why they so powerfully witness to the divine love poured into our hearts (see Romans 5:5).

Andrew: When it comes to chastity, I can vividly remember the reaction of several of my college football buddies during my conversion when I told them I was leaving my old relationship for reasons of purity. They admitted that, while they would never have made such a decision, they had immense respect for me in doing so. Several guys on the team said things like, "Dude, you're like the best guy I've ever met," solely because they couldn't ever imagine themselves or anyone they knew having the strength to do such a thing. It was clear to them that this wasn't the "easy" way out—they knew there was something *different* here.

The same is true of real forgiveness, where we cease to hold the other person in our debt—where we cease to project the past upon the present (see Colossians 3:12–13). As we noted, forgiveness does not mean forgetting the past, nor does it mean no longer having strong feelings about it. But it does mean we surrender our right to hold the other person in our debt for having wronged us; it means letting go of this debt and no longer "keeping score." Such forgiveness is not natural or normal. The normal response is to defend our ego and our "rights" at all costs, vigorously keeping track of all those who have wronged us and the extent to which they still "owe" us.

But if we are a people of Christ's victory over sin and death, of what or whom should we be afraid (see Psalm 27:1)?

If we are truly people of the resurrection, why would we seek to defend our "rights" at all costs, since all is gift in the end?

This is what it means to be touched by the risen Christ and to have accepted his invitation to go all in with him. It means we live with one foot in the current age and one already now in the age to come.

It means we *live with eternity in mind*—with a holy fearlessness and boldness.

This is the *difference* Christ makes.

CONCLUSION

We have been on quite a ride.

One of the amazing things about Christianity is that it thoroughly taps into the human experience and answers the deepest human questions. For one, it answers our most fundamental of fears—namely, the fear of death and being thoroughly forgotten.

We are known and loved by the Lord of all creation. He has defeated death once and for all in the cross and resurrection of Jesus Christ.

Without faith, many today spend their lives in search of *meaning* and *purpose*, seeking to find it in relationships with a significant other, in a career, or some other endeavor—grasping at anything that might numb or distract them from their despair.

The truth is *we long for meaning.*

The secret to living a fully meaningful life is to recognize *gift* at the heart of it all. We have been loved into existence and given a part to play in this great story by the Divine Director. Once we see this, we realize that life is no longer about *grasping, controlling,* or *manipulating* situations in the hope of getting what we want.

When we realize that gift is at the heart of it all, this changes how we think about our friendships, relationships, or the parts of our life that have not gone as we had hoped or planned. Recognizing that true meaning is *received* helps us to be open to God surprising us, and it helps us place our sufferings and toils in a deeper perspective.

It helps us realize that our lives are not our own—that we have been created and "bought with a price" (1 Corinthians 6:20). We have been claimed and redeemed by a God who loves us and has a plan for us.

When we know these truths deeply within our hearts, not only does our life take on a whole new meaning, but we begin to make our lives a gift for others.

This is the path to healing and growth, which does not come without effort. It begins and ends with Jesus—sharing in his cross and resurrection.

If we join with others who want to live on mission, forming our own *Środowisko*, we will find ourselves inspired and supported by friends who are united in their pursuit of Jesus Christ—an experience that transforms friendship, dating, and marriage.

If we live *Środowisko* with heroic virtue, our lives will never be the same.

Going *all in* with the Lord is the only thing that makes sense.

Undoubtedly this will "cost" something; but the pearl of great price is more than worth it—both in this life and the next.

When people run together in this way, the chains of fear and isolation are broken—and the rays of divine love and hope pierce our hearts, infusing us with meaning and sustaining us with supernatural grit.

Not only will we live a life of peace, joy, and confidence, but the impact of our lives will be felt for years to come, in ways we cannot even fathom. This will be our legacy, both in time and eternity.

This was our experience when we met the Lord in a profound way many years ago in college. It was the experience of our students during our semester abroad in Florence, and the same is true of countless others with whom we have walked over the years.

You are not alone.

Catching fire with the love of Jesus and doing so with a group of people running toward him with meaning and purpose changes everything.

We know this journey is not easy, but it is so worth it.

We thank you for allowing us to be part of your *Środowisko*.

In a special way, we pray for your discernment of the Lord's will for you and eagerly await the part you will play (and are already playing) in this divine story—a part that would never be the same without you ... *your gift and your grit.*

Your life matters—far more than you'll ever realize.

You are seen, known, and loved.

Be assured of our prayers for you,

Dr. Andrew and Sarah Swafford

DISCUSSION QUESTIONS

INTRODUCTION

1. What do you think gives rise to feelings of isolation, worthlessness, and lack of direction and purpose for people today? How prevalent do you think this is? Have you ever experienced any of these feelings yourself? Explain.

2. How does social media contribute to the feelings described above? Do you think some forms of social media are more prone than others to increase our sense of dissatisfaction with life? Why or why not?

3. How is life a journey, especially in terms of our becoming a certain kind of person along the way? Explain.

4. Who in your life has shaped you the most? Discuss how and why.

5. What makes you "tired" with life? What makes you come alive and why?

CHAPTER 1: WOUNDS—WHY THIS WILL NOT BE EASY

1. How does our desire to be *seen*, *known*, and *loved* manifest in our lives? Explain.

2. What are you afraid of? Is there anything in your own story that might play into your specific fears? Explain.

3. How are the wounds of men and women similar? How are they different and why?

CHAPTER 2: OUR STORIES

1. While everybody's story is unique, which of our stories resonates most with you and why?

2. Is there anything in your life you turn to as a "crutch," supporting your sense of self-worth and identity? What connections do you see here between your various "crutches" and what we discussed earlier in the previous chapter on wounds? Explain.

3. Do you have any abrupt moments in your story— emphatic "before" and "after" moments—that were decisive for the direction of your life? Explain.

4. Do you think that one's conversion story is ever fully "finished"? Do you think there can be both distinctive moments that stand out, and yet still an ongoing story that continues to unfold throughout our lives? How do these dynamics of conversion resonate with your own story? Explain.

5. Are there people in your life that have played a similar role to those in our stories? (For example, friends or family members who pointed the way to Christ, a particular priest, teacher, or youth minister or campus minister who was especially influential for you, etc.) What stands out in how they became a witness of Christ for you? Explain.

CHAPTER 3: WHAT IS *ŚRODOWISKO* ("SHRO-DO-VEE-SKOH")?

1. What do you think of Václav Havel's greengrocer parable? Do you ever feel like there is a "publicly accepted" view of things? Does this ever make you feel like you need to keep quiet about your faith or what you really think? How so? Explain.

2. What stands out about the friendships within the *Środowisko* community? How vital do you think it was for them to have each other? How do you think going up to the mountains together and removing themselves from the heart of the communistic culture within Krakow helped in this regard? Do you ever feel the need for something similar? Explain.

3. What does it mean for a community to gather "for a purpose," with intentionality? Do you think that a purpose-driven community can also have a good time together? Do you think both elements (having fun and having purpose) are important? How so? Explain.

4. What would it mean for you to form a *Środowisko* of your own? How do you think it would benefit you, and how would you go about forming such a group?

CHAPTER 4: WHERE DO WE FIND MEANING?

1. How is the deepest *meaning* of our lives related to gift, as in the *gift* of our lives? What do you think of the statement that "self-made meaning" is no meaning at all? Explain.

2. How do you think busyness plays into our sense of an *absence* of genuine meaning in our lives? Have you ever experienced this? How so? Explain.

3. What do you make of our temptation to compare our "behind the scenes" to everyone else's "highlight reel"? How can this become a "thief of joy"? Explain.

4. How does seeing our life as intimately wrapped up in the drama of creation, sin, and redemption change how we view its meaning? How does believing we are here for a reason, with a distinct part to play in the divine story, enhance our sense of meaning and purpose?

CHAPTER 5: WHAT IF MEANING ALONE IS NOT ENOUGH?

1. In what way do you think grit is necessary to succeed in life? Have you ever experienced having *meaning* but lacking *grit*? What happens when this is the case?

2. How does our sense of meaning bolster our grit? If we lose our sense of meaning and purpose, why does it become more difficult to persevere and sustain our grit? Does this resonate with your experience? Explain.

3. In what sense is freedom the "ability to do the good"? How is the moral and spiritual life analogous to that of an athlete or anyone who sets out to master a craft (e.g., language or music)? In this sense, how does one's freedom *increase* over time with practice and discipline? Have you experienced this? Explain.

4. Is authentic happiness merely the result of what happens *to* us? Or does it have more to do with who we are becoming on the inside, that is, our character? What does this mean to you? Explain.

5. What is distinctive about *supernatural* grit? How does maintaining one's peace and joy, even amidst trial, figure in here? What convictions become an important source of maintaining one's peace and joy even through trial?

Do you find that hope of heaven and a sense that this life is not our ultimate end are important here? How so?

6. Without naming any individuals, can you think of people in your life who (a) have a deep sense of meaning but not grit; (b) have serious grit but lack meaning; and (c) have both a deep sense of meaning and heroic grit? Do you see any patterns among those who have one or the other but not both? Which of the two—meaning or grit—is more typically lacking in your experience? Of the people in your life who have both, what are they like? Describe them.

CHAPTER 6: HOW DO I NAVIGATE NEW AND OLD FRIENDSHIPS?

1. One of the best ways to grow in virtue is simply to spend a lot of time with virtuous people. In your experience, how do people rub off on each other over time? For example, have you ever noticed that when friends spend a lot of time together, they begin to take on each other's mannerisms, use similar expressions, and even talk like one another? If friends rub off on each other even in these small ways, how can they affect the formation of our character overall? What does this mean to you? Explain.

2. Do you notice that the deeper the realities you and your friends have in common, the deeper are your friendships? How does this affect the nature and depth of your conversations? Does this affect which friends you go to for advice? How does this affect what we are looking for in our closest friends? Explain.

3. If it is true that our deepest friendships will be with those with whom we have the deepest things in common, how important is it to have friends who share

our faith? Is there a correlation between how important our faith is to us and how important we think it is to cultivate friendships with people who share our faith? How so? Explain.

4. As we get older, how does what we love and cherish become an important basis for friendship? Have you had the experience of a common love (love of the same thing) bringing people together and uniting them? Explain.

CHAPTER 7: I KNOW GOOD FRIENDS ARE CRUCIAL, BUT *HOW* DO I MAKE THEM?

1. How does "living on mission" help in forming deeper friendships? Have you experienced anything like this? Explain.

2. How do deep, virtuous friendships connect on "all levels"? Have you witnessed or experienced friendships that click on one level but not others? In what ways were these friendships limited by not being able to connect on all levels? Explain.

3. How is taking an interest in other people's lives an act of charity and selflessness? Do you find this to be an attractive trait in others? How do you respond when someone seems to be too into themselves and not very interested in your life? How might this motivate us to be more interested and invested in the lives of others? Explain.

4. In your experience, how do *availability, vulnerability,* and *accountability* play into the depth of your friendships? Why are these sometimes difficult to live out? What are the benefits of having all three ingredients present and active in a friendship? Have you experienced this

before? Which ingredient is typically lacking in your experience and why do you think that is?

5. How do conversations with your good friends about the nature of virtuous friendship help make availability, vulnerability, and accountability more of a reality in your friendships? Why is it harder to make these three ingredients a reality if you've never discussed them with your friends? Explain.

6. If loving means *willing the other's good*, what are the implications for friendship? Is our good solely defined by how we feel in the moment or what we might want—or is there more to it? Explain.

CHAPTER 8: CAN MEN AND WOMEN BE FRIENDS?

1. In your experience, how are men and women similar? How are they different?

2. How can these differences contribute to the potential pitfalls of male-female friendship? How can these differences help our growth in virtue? Explain.

3. How does a man grow in his ability to love by having authentic female friends? How does a woman grow in her ability to love by having genuine male friends? In what ways are we negatively impacted when such authentic friendships are lacking?

4. How does living on mission help curb pitfalls in male-female friendships and bring out their beauty and goodness in powerful and healthy ways? Explain.

5. Why are men and women living on mission together a wonderful context to begin romantic relationships? At the same time, how does living on mission *solely for the sake of finding a romantic partner* undermine everything we are trying to build by living on mission? Explain.

CHAPTER 9: WHO SHOULD I DATE AND HOW DO I GO ABOUT IT?

1. What are some problems with seeking happiness and fulfillment solely through a dating relationship? How does this actually set the relationship up to fail? Explain. Have you ever experienced this or seen it among people you know? Explain.

2. What is a "friendship in motion"? Can this friendship stay as it is forever? Have you ever experienced or witnessed this type of friendship? How would you describe it? Were you able to recognize it as it was happening or only after the fact? Is it easier to recognize this type of friendship for what it is when it's happening with *other* people? Why is this? Explain.

3. Why is "settling" in a relationship a bad idea? On the other side, what might it mean to be "too picky"? Have you ever seen or experienced either one of these? Explain.

4. What do you think keeps good people from asking each other out on dates? How can we overcome this hesitation? Do you have any practical ideas? Explain.

5. What does it mean to "define the relationship"? What are its two distinct stages? In your opinion, how much time should elapse between the first and second stages? What happens when too much time goes by between the two stages and how can that lead to confusion and hurt? Does this resonate with your experience? Explain.

6. How can pursuing more than one person at a time compromise "sincerity" and "clarity"? What often results when things aren't clear? Does this resonate with your experience? How so?

7. Why are God, chemistry, and timing so important for the development and formation of a strong relationship? Have you ever had the experience (or witnessed it in someone else) where some of these were present but not all? What was it like? Explain.

CHAPTER 10: BREAKUPS CAN BE BRUTAL—HOW CAN I MOVE ON WHEN I KEEP LOOKING BACK?

1. Is it a good idea to maintain a close friendship with an ex immediately after a breakup? How does the dating process affect our ability to be friends afterward? Discuss the need for a period of *not* being friends immediately after breaking up. What has been your experience in this area, either personally or with people you have known? Explain.

2. What are the important keys for moving on after a breakup? What do we need to remind ourselves of during this painful time? Why is this the case and how can it help? Explain. In your experience (or that of your friends), which of the keys have you found most difficult to live out and why? Explain.

3. Discuss why it might have been good for two people to have dated, even if they ended up breaking up. How does this affect or change your view of dating and its purpose? Explain.

4. How was Jan Tyranowski able to immerse himself in the present—in the specific mission God had for him? If his mind and heart were preoccupied with what he didn't have, would he have been ready to answer the Lord's call in the way he did? How can you apply this to your life? Explain.

CHAPTER 11: CHASTITY IS CRUCIAL—
BUT WHY IS IT SO DANG DIFFICULT?

1. Are temptations against chastity difficult at any age or do they go away as one gets older? How might one's age affect their answer here? Explain.

2. Is chastity the friend or foe of love? How does our answer to this question affect how we view love (and vice versa)? Explain.

3. Discuss the challenge of love—of putting the objective good of the other person ahead of our own personal desires. Have you experienced the temptation to put your *experience* above the objective good of the other person? Even if our actions *feel* very loving, how can they actually be an instance of putting ourselves first? Explain. Can our *feelings* be at odds with the truth? Explain. Have you ever experienced this? What was it like? Explain.

4. How does a failure in chastity lead us to use the other person, even if our actions feel loving? How does chastity free us from using? If someone is willing to fight this battle for you, what does this say about their ability to sacrifice for you? If they're willing to give this up for you, is there anything they *can't* do for you? What do you think? Explain your thoughts here.

5. Regarding the six keys to success in chastity, do you think most people believe that victory is possible here with God's help, or do you think they assume defeat from the beginning? Explain the danger in believing the battle is already lost before we begin. Which of these six keys do you find to be the most important for you to succeed in your journey? Explain. What are your biggest challenges in this area and which of the six keys

is the hardest for you to fully implement and live out? Explain.

6. How important is it to have friends supporting and challenging us in chastity? How do you think the three ingredients of virtuous friendship—availability, vulnerability, accountability—come into play here? What is your experience with friends in this regard? What do you hope for in your future friendships in this area? How might living on mission affect the nature of our friendships and our ability to succeed with regard to purity and chastity? Explain.

CHAPTER 12: WHAT DOES SEX HAVE TO DO WITH THE SPIRITUAL LIFE?

1. How does sex—in temptation or shame for past sins— often keep us from fully experiencing God's love? Explain. How does this resonate with your experience or that of your friends?

2. Does the "B.L.A.S.T." acronym resonate with your experience? How so? Explain.

3. What is sloth? What outlets are we tempted to seek when we suffer from sloth? Does this resonate with your experience? Explain.

4. What is the difference between *striving* for holiness and being spiritually *lukewarm*? How can this make all the difference? Do you find this distinction helpful? Explain your answer.

CHAPTER 13: WHAT DOES IT MEAN TO GO *ALL IN* WITH THE LORD?

1. Is there an episode in your life that "haunted" you, similar to Sarah's experience with the young man who

wore the Jesus T-shirt at the concert? In your own words, what does it mean to be seen *with* Jesus? What does it mean to be fully seen *by* him? What makes this difficult? Explain.

2. Does the story of the rich young man resonate with your experience? Are there times in your life when you were afraid to hand something over to the Lord? Is this true of anything in your life now? What can help you overcome this fear? Explain.

3. How does prayer help in overcoming fear? Have you ever had the experience in prayer of receiving greater *clarity* as to what you need to do and increased *strength* to do what you were afraid to do? Explain.

4. Why is "self-deception" easy to fall into? How does prayer help bring self-deception to light, especially when it comes to rationalizing and justifying our behavior? Have you or your friends ever had this experience— of prayer convicting you of something you should or shouldn't be doing? Explain.

5. Why is mental prayer so powerful in unmasking self-deception? Why is it difficult to persist in this kind of prayer *and* serious sin? Explain and draw from your own experience if you can.

6. What are the four pillars that can help secure our spiritual growth and progress? Which do you find most challenging and why? Explain.

7. What does it mean for Jesus to be "Lord of your entire mind and heart"? How can this be both *scary* and *exciting*? Explain.

CHAPTER 14: I KNOW I NEED HEALING, BUT WHERE DO I BEGIN?

I. Why do we need healing? How does healing affect both ourselves and others? Explain. Does this resonate with your experience? Explain.

2. What are the steps we need to take to begin healing? Explain.

3. Why is prayer essential in allowing Jesus to truly heal us in the deepest of ways? How is prayer like "sitting in the sun"? Explain.

4. What does it mean to be "emotionally naked" before the Lord in prayer? Does this sound scary? Does it also sound safe and comforting—to be loved as you are? How is this a lifelong journey? Explain your answer.

CHAPTER 15: HOW DO I DEAL WITH MY PAIN?

I. What does it mean to surrender our past into the arms of the Lord?

2. Why does forgiveness not necessarily include reconciliation? Are there any examples in your life where the Lord may be calling you to forgive, whether reconciliation is likely to happen or not? Have you ever seen this in others? Explain.

3. How does Fr. Walter Ciszek embody the concept of supernatural grit? How does he embody the importance of living a life of meaning and grit, and how was his sense of meaning connected to his grit? Explain. What can we learn from him and apply to our lives today?

4. Discuss the quote from Witold Pilecki. What does it mean to live with eternity in mind? How does this affect our outlook on life?

CHAPTER 16: HOW DO I LIVE WITH ETERNITY IN MIND?

1. What things reveal what is truly most important in our lives? Does this change how we view what it means to really put God first? Which aspects of this chapter resonate the most with you? Which do you find most challenging and why? Explain.

2. How is evangelization an act of love? What makes evangelization sometimes scary? Discuss any tips for evangelization presented in this chapter that you found particularly helpful. Explain.

3. What are some of the "undeniable witnesses" presented in this chapter? Does this resonate with your experience? Explain.

4. How is Christianity about far more than just being a "nice person"? What is the *difference* that Christ makes? What does this mean to you? Explain.

CONCLUSION

1. What does it mean to go "all in" with the Lord and how does this change everything about our lives—including and especially our relationships?

2. What do you take away from this book that you hope stays with you for the rest of your life?

3. How has this book changed your perspective on friendships, dating relationships, and even your future marriage (or your marriage now if you are already married)? Once we have truly encountered Christ, are we ever the same again? How so? Explain.

4. How can our stories of being touched by Christ become instruments for others to receive this same transformative gift? How do you think you can best

share your story with others? Explain. Perhaps practice different versions of your story (e.g., one minute, three-to-five minutes, and longer versions) and share with your group if you feel comfortable.

ACKNOWLEDGMENTS

We wish to thank all those countless people—students, friends, and mentors—who over the years have shared life with us and talked with us about many of the themes found in this book. Sharing life with you has shaped us in so many ways, and we are so grateful.

We also want to thank Hadleigh Thomas of Ascension for her oversight of this project and for her encouragement and guidance along the way, as well as Mike Flickinger and Meredith Wilson for their editorial help— and Jennifer Eckenrode and the entire Ascension team. Thank you for using your many talents for our Lord and the Church.

In a special way, we express our deep gratitude to those who reviewed draft versions of the manuscript and gave us vital feedback. We were so moved by the zeal of this incredible group and are grateful that some of the readers were even among the original *Środowisko* with us in Florence: Grayson and Laura Feist, Michael and Sydney Shanahan, Mark and Maisy Williams (these are the three marriages mentioned earlier from our time in Florence!), Miguel Rodriguez, Fr. John Burns, Fr. Craig Vasek, Bobby and Jackie Angel, Mary Margaret Mulvaney, Liza Trettel, Kayla Arpin, Reese Holder, Madi Abbot, James O'Neil, Andrew Laubacher, David

O'Neill, Caden Bennett, Madeleine Sri, Joe Muti, and Justin Honeywell. You guys are seriously the best!

As always, we thank our families for their loving support. In a special way, we thank our children—Thomas, Fulton, Cate, Kolbe, John Paul, and our littlest one in the womb. Without their help and patience while we were poring over the manuscript, this book would never have seen the light of day. We love you guys, and we are so proud of you—you continue to be our inspiration and joy! We would especially like to thank our eldest sons, Thomas and Fulton, who also read the manuscript in advance and gave us terrific feedback from a teenage vantage point!

Lastly, we thank Almighty God, in whom we live and move and have our very being (see Acts 17:28), who gave us his only Son that we may have *life* and have it abundantly (see John 10:10). May this work glorify him and lead others to see him as the sure and steady anchor of their lives and their ultimate end, in whom alone our hearts will finally come to rest.

ABOUT THE AUTHORS

Dr. Andrew and Sarah Swafford are international speakers on dating, marriage, the moral and spiritual life, St. John Paul II, and Sacred Scripture. They are cohosts of *What We Believe: The Beauty of the Catholic Faith* from Ascension. Sarah is also author of *Emotional Virtue: A Guide to Drama-Free Relationships* and contributor to Ascension's *Chosen*. Andrew is a professor of theology at Benedictine College and a general editor of *The Great Adventure Catholic Bible*. He is also cohost of Ascension's studies *Romans: The Gospel of Salvation* and *Hebrews: The New and Eternal Covenant*; author of several books, including *John Paul II to Aristotle and Back Again: A Christian Philosophy of Life*; and coauthor of *What We Believe: The Beauty of the Catholic Faith*. Andrew and Sarah live in Atchison, Kansas, with their six children.

NOTES

1. See Sarah Swafford, *Emotional Virtue: A Guide to Drama-Free Relationships* (Lakewood, CO: Totus Tuus Press, 2014), 78.

2. George Weigel, *Witness to Hope: The Biography of Pope John Paul II* (New York: HarperCollins, 1999), 46, 52.

3. Weigel, 97.

4. Václav Havel, *The Power of the Powerless*, trans. Paul Wilson (London: Vintage, 2018), 14–15. (The original publication date was 1978.)

5. See George Weigel, *The Final Revolution: The Resistance Church and the Collapse of Communism* (New York: Oxford University Press, 1992), 41.

6. Weigel, *Witness to Hope*, 102–103.

7. Weigel, 100. The quote is from an interview with an original *Środowisko* member.

8. Weigel, 105. The quote is from an interview with a *Środowisko* member.

9. Weigel, 105, emphasis added.

10. John Paul II, *Crossing the Threshold of Hope*, ed. Vittorio Messori (New York: Alfred A. Knopf, 1994), 123, emphasis added.

11. John Paul II, 123.

12. See Joseph Ratzinger, *Introduction to Christianity*, trans. J.R. Foster (San Francisco: Ignatius, 1990), 43.

13. For explanations regarding God's existence, see Andrew Dean Swafford, *John Paul II to Aristotle and Back Again: A Christian Philosophy of Life* (Eugene, OR: Wipf and Stock, 2015), 1–14, and Stephen M. Barr, *Modern Physics and Ancient Faith* (Notre Dame, IN: University of Notre Dame Press, 2003), 65–92, 118–137.

14. J.R.R. Tolkien, *The Lord of the Rings* (Boston: Houghton Mifflin, 1987), 51, emphasis added.

15. See Aquinas, *Summa Theologiae* II-IIae.123.6, II-IIae.128.1 ad 4 and 5.

16. C.S. Lewis, *The Screwtape Letters* (San Francisco: HarperCollins, 1996), 162, emphasis added.

17. See Jocko Willink, *Discipline Equals Freedom: Field Manual MK1-MOD1* (New York: St. Martin's Press, 2020).

18. For more here, see Swafford, *John Paul II to Aristotle and Back Again*, 28–29.

19. Swafford, *John Paul II to Aristotle and Back Again*, 28–29.

20. See Swafford, *John Paul II to Aristotle and Back Again*, 23–26.

21. See Sarah Swafford, "We Are Women at the Well," in *Women Made New!*, ed. Crystalina Evert (Irondale, AL: EWTN Publishing, 2022), 163–172.

22. See Angela Duckworth, *Grit: The Power of Passion and Perseverance* (New York: Scribner, 2016).

23. See Evagrius Ponticus, *The Praktikos and Chapters on Prayer*, trans. John Eudes Bamberger (Kalamazoo, MI: Cistercian Publications, 1981), 17–20, and St. John Climacus, *The Ladder of Divine Ascent*, trans. Lazarus Moore (New York: Missionary Society of St. Paul, 1982), 87–89. See also Brant Pitre, *Introduction to the Spiritual Life: Walking the Path of Prayer with Jesus* (New York: Image, 2021), 185–186.

24. This is the thrust of St. Ignatius' "rule 5" in overcoming desolation. See Timothy M. Gallagher, *The Discernment of Spirits: An Ignatian Guide for Everyday Living* (New York: Crossroad, 2005), 74–80.

25. John Paul II, *Familiaris Consortio* (November 22, 1981), 75, 86.

26. See Aristotle, *Nicomachean Ethics* 8.3, cited from *Aristotle: Nicomachean Ethics*, trans. Terence Irwin (Indianapolis, IN: Hackett Publishing, 1999), 122.

27. Andrew Dean Swafford, *Spiritual Survival in the Modern World: Insights from C.S. Lewis's* Screwtape Letters (Eugene, OR: Wipf and Stock, 2016), 54–58. See also C.S. Lewis, *The Screwtape Letters* (San Francisco: HarperCollins, 2001), 70–73, and C.S. Lewis, *Mere Christianity* (San Francisco: HarperCollins, 2001), 125, 128. See also Rick Warren, *The Purpose Driven Life* (Grand Rapids, MI: Zondervan, 2012), 262, emphasis altered.

28. See *Nicomachean Ethics* 1.13.

29. Karol Wojtyła, *Love and Responsibility*, trans. Grzegorz Ignatik (Boston, MA: Pauline Books and Media, 2013), 87–96. This translation uses "affectivity" in place of "sentimentality," which is found in the older English translation. See Karol Wojtyła, *Love and Responsibility*, trans. H.T. Willetts (San Francisco: Ignatius, 1993), 104–113. See also Swafford, *John Paul II to Aristotle and Back Again*, 54–61.

30. Wojtyła, *Love and Responsibility*, trans. Ignatik, 257–258.

31. Cited in Ryan T. Anderson, *When Harry Became Sally: Responding to the Transgender Moment* (New York: Encounter Books, 2018), 164.

32. See Wojtyła, *Love and Responsibility*, 12–15.

33. Wojtyła, 147, emphasis added.

34. Wojtyła, 95.

35. Sarah Swafford, *Emotional Virtue*, 115–122.

36. Swafford, *Emotional Virtue*, 115–122.

37. See Wojtyła, *Love and Responsibility*, 90, 96, 121.

38. See Wojtyła, 105.

39. Wojtyła, 121.

40. See Swafford, *Emotional Virtue*, 115–121, 131–137.

41. See Swafford, *Emotional Virtue*, 125–147.

42. Andrew Swafford, *Spiritual Survival in the Modern World*, 11–18, 119–125.

43. Weigel, *Witness to Hope*, 60, 81.

44. Weigel, 61. See also Andrew Swafford, "A Fight for the Soul: Venerable Jan Tyranowski's Spiritual Resistance in Nazi-Occupied Poland," *Word Among Us* (February 2019): 53–64.

45. Wojtyła, *Love and Responsibility*, 147, emphasis added.

46. See Sarah Swafford, *Emotional Virtue*, 151–152, and Andrew Swafford, *John Paul II to Aristotle and Back Again*, 60–61. See also Wojtyła, *Love and Responsibility*, 155.

47. Wojtyła, 154. See also Andrew Swafford, *John Paul II to Aristotle and Back Again*, 60–61.

48. See Christopher West, *Good News About Sex and Marriage: Answers to Your Honest Questions About Catholic Teaching* (Cincinnati: Servant Books, 2000), 76.

49. Matt Fradd, *Delivered: True Stories of Men and Women Who Turned from Porn to Purity* (San Diego: Catholic Answers Press, 2013).

50. Augustine, *Confessions* 8.7.

51. Lewis, *Mere Christianity*, 101–102.

52. This quote has been attributed to both St. Augustine and St. Ignatius of Loyola.

53. C.S. Lewis, *The Magician's Nephew* (New York: Scholastic, 1988), 18.

54. See Swafford, *John Paul II to Aristotle and Back Again*, 44.

55. Francis, *Evangelii Gaudium* (November 24, 2013), 3, emphasis added.

56. Aquinas, *Summa Theologiae* I.20.3.

57. Gregory K. Popcak, *Holy Sex! A Catholic Guide to Toe-Curling, Mind-Blowing, Infallible Loving* (New York: Crossroad Publishing, 2008), 164.

58. See Jean-Charles Nault, *The Noonday Devil: Acedia, the Unnamed Evil of Our Times*, trans. Michael J. Miller (San Francisco: Ignatius, 2015), 27–28.

59. Aquinas, *Summa Theologiae* II-IIae.35.1.

60. Aquinas II-IIae.35.4.

61. See Swafford, *John Paul II to Aristotle and Back Again*, 43.

62. See John Paul II, *Veritatis Splendor* (August 6, 1993), 69–70, 78. A mortal sin is an action that is incompatible with authentic love of God, neighbor, or even ourselves. The Ten Commandments are the starting point for the Church's reflection as to what constitutes a grave or mortal sin (see CCC 1858).

63. Lewis, *Screwtape Letters*, 61. See Swafford, *Spiritual Survival in the Modern World*, 40–46.

64. John Paul II, *Crossing the Threshold of Hope*, 123, emphasis added.

65. The professor's name is Robert George. See Robert P. George (@McCormickProf), "1/ I sometimes ask students what their position on slavery would have been," Twitter post, July 1, 2020, https://twitter.com/mccormickprof/status/127852969435529216.

66. Of course, this is not to say that we necessarily *should* drive if we've had a few drinks and are still below the legal limit.

67. Sarah Swafford, *Emotional Virtue*, 129.

68. See Andrew Swafford and Jeff Cavins, *Romans: The Gospel of Salvation* (West Chester, PA: Ascension, 2019).

69. See Bob Schuchts, *Be Healed: A Guide to Encountering the Powerful Love of Jesus in Your Life* (Notre Dame, IN: Ave Maria Press, 2014), 87–126, and Miriam James Heidland, *Loved As I Am: An Invitation to Conversion, Healing, and Freedom Through Jesus* (Notre Dame, IN: Ave Maria Press, 2014).

70. See Aaron Kheriaty with John Cihak, *The Catholic Guide to Depression: How the Saints, the Sacraments, and Psychiatry Can Help You Break Its Grip and Find Happiness Again* (Manchester, NH: Sophia, 2012).

71. See Jacques Philippe, *Interior Freedom*, trans. Helena Scott (New York: Scepter, 2002), 44–45.

72. See Scott Stanley, Daniel Trathen, Savanna McCain, and Milt Bryan, *A Lasting Promise: A Christian Guide to Fighting for Your Marriage* (San Francisco: Jossey-Bass, 2002), 203–213.

73. Walter J. Ciszek, *With God in Russia* (New York: HarperOne, 2017), 9.

74. Ciszek, 21.

75. Ciszek, 31–33.

76. Walter J. Ciszek, *He Leadeth Me* (New York: Image, 1973), 181–182, emphasis added.

77. Ciszek, 132–133, emphasis added.

78. Ciszek, *With God in Russia*, 382. After serving his fifteen-year sentence, he spent several years under "house arrest" in Russia, where he was closely monitored and very restricted as to where he could go. Needless to say, he was not permitted to leave the country.

79. This phrase literally means "remember to die," but the sense of the phrase is to keep the reality of death before one's mind.

80. See George Weigel, *The End and the Beginning: Pope John Paul II— The Victory of Freedom, the Last Years, the Legacy* (New York: Image, 2010), 24–27.

81. Marcellino D'Ambrosio and Andrew Swafford, *What We Believe: The Beauty of the Catholic Faith* (West Chester, PA: Ascension, 2022), 189–190.

82. Lewis, *Mere Christianity*, 141.

83. Sherry A. Weddell, *Forming Intentional Disciples: The Path to Knowing and Following Jesus* (Huntington, IN: Our Sunday Visitor, 2012), 161–162.

Also from **Ascension**

Catholic Bible

The Catholic Bible That **Teaches You** How to **Read** It

With commentary from the creator of The Great Adventure®, *Jeff Cavins, and renowned Scripture scholars Mary Healy, Andrew Swafford, and Peter Williamson*

Every Catholic needs this Bible! *The Great Adventure Catholic Bible* makes the complexity of reading the Bible simple. The narrative approach gives the big picture of salvation history and shows how everything ties together. This is the only Bible that incorporates *The Great Adventure's* color-coded *Bible Timeline®* Learning System, a system that has made *The Great Adventure* the most popular and influential Bible study program in the English-speaking world. The color-coded tools make it easy to read and easy to remember. *Also available in Spanish.*

ascensionpress.com

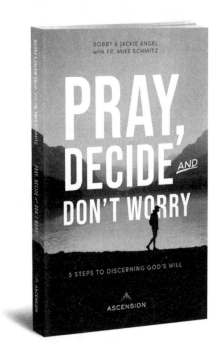